CHURCH
POLITICS

CHURCH
POLITICS

Keith R. Bridston

The World Publishing Company

NEW YORK AND CLEVELAND

Published by The World Publishing Company
2231 West 110th Street, Cleveland, Ohio 44102

Published simultaneously in Canada by
Nelson, Foster & Scott Ltd.

First Printing — 1969

Manufactured at World Publishing Press,
a division of The World Publishing Company, Cleveland, Ohio
Library of Congress Catalog Card Number: 70-84549

PRINTED IN THE UNITED STATES OF AMERICA

WORLD PUBLISHING
TIMES MIRROR

Acknowledgment is gratefully made to the following
for permission to quote from the sources indicated.

THE AMERICAN LUTHERAN CHURCH

From President's Column, by Frederick A. Schiotz in *Commentator,* August 1966. Reprinted with permission.

THE ASSOCIATED PRESS

"Pope Urges Faith in Church Dogma," an Associated Press release from Vatican City. Copyright 1968. Reprinted with permission.

ATHENEUM PUBLISHERS

From *Human Aggression* by Anthony Storr. Copyright © 1968 by Anthony Storr. Reprinted by permission of Atheneum. Publisher.

CHICAGO SUN-TIMES

"Parishioners Protest Calendar Shift," by Hugh Hough, issue of January 20, 1968. Copyright 1968. Reprinted with permission from the *Chicago Sun-Times.*

DAEDALUS

From "The 'New Breed' in American Churches," by Harvey Cox, copyright 1967. Reprinted by permission from *Daedalus,* Journal of the American Academy of Arts and Sciences, Boston, Massachusetts.

DOUBLEDAY & COMPANY, INC.

From *Community, State, and Church,* by Karl Barth. © 1960 by The National Student Christian Federation. Reprinted by permission.

FOREIGN AFFAIRS

From "One Thing We Learned," by Bill D. Moyers, vol. 46, no. 4 (July, 1968). Reprinted with permission.

HARPER & ROW, PUBLISHERS, INCORPORATED
From *Synectics,* by William J. J. Gordon. Copyright 1961. Reprinted with permission.

HORIZON PRESS
From *Frank Lloyd Wright: Writings and Buildings,* selected by Edgar Kaufmann and Ben Raeburn. Copyright 1960. Reprinted by permission of the publisher.

NEW YORK TIMES
From "Case for Bureaucracy: Exposing 6 Myths," by Harland Cleveland, November 1, 1967. © 1967 by The New York Times Company. Reprinted by permission.
From an article by B. A. Cortesi, June 12, 1963. © 1963 by The New York Times Company. Reprinted by permission.
From an article by Edward B. Fiske, April 28, 1968. © 1968 by The New York Times Company. Reprinted by permission.
"Impasse in Texas Catholic Revolt." © 1968 by The New York Times Company. Reprinted by permission.

NEWSPAPER ENTERPRISE ASSOCIATION INC.
"Mae West Raps Modern Bedtime Movies," (NEA) *Berkeley* (California) *Daily Gazette.* Copyright 1968.

OUR SUNDAY VISITOR, INC., and CANON LAW SOCIETY OF AMERICA
From *We, the People of God: A Study of Constitutional Government for the Church,* edited by James A. Coriden. Copyright © 1968 by Our Sunday Visitor, Inc., and Canon Law Society of America. Reprinted by permission.

OXFORD UNIVERSITY PRESS
From *Love, Power and Justice,* by Paul Tillich. Copyright 1960. Reprinted with permission.

PAULIST-NEWMAN PRESS and GEOFFREY CHAPMAN LIMITED
From *Lay People in the Church,* by Yves M.-J. Congar. Copyright 1957.

PRISM PUBLICATIONS
From "Spotlight on Uppsala." Reprinted with permission from *New Christian,* July 25, 1968.

THE HERBERT READ DISCRETIONARY TRUST
From *The Meaning of Art* by Sir Herbert Read, published by Faber & Faber, Ltd. Copyright 1949. Used with permission.

REUTERS
"A Priests' Rebellion in Germany," a Reuters press release from Bonn, West Germany. Copyright 1968. Used with permission.

SHEED & WARD INC.
From *The Christian Commitment,* by Karl Rahner, S.J. © Sheed & Ward Ltd., 1963. Published in England by Sheed & Ward as *The Council and Reunion and Mission and Grace,* Volume I.
From *The Council, Reform and Reunion,* by Hans Küng. © Sheed & Ward Ltd., 1963.

TIMES NEWSPAPERS LIMITED, LONDON
"Vatican Attacks 'Foolhardy' Critics," *The Times,* August 14, 1968. Reprinted with permission.

UNITED PRESS INTERNATIONAL
"Congregation Beat Him, Declares Minister," (UPI) release from Blytheville, Ark. Copyright 1968. Reprinted with permission.

THE VIKING PRESS INC. and HUTCHINSON & CO. LTD.
From *On Power: Its Nature and the History of Its Growth,* by Bertrand de Jouvenel, trans. J. F. Huntington. Copyright 1962.

YALE UNIVERSITY PRESS
From *Essay On Man,* by Ernst Cassirer, copyright 1944; and *Language and Myth* by Ernst Cassirer, copyright 1946. Reprinted with permission of Yale University Press.

In Memory of My Father
Joseph B. Bridston 1896 - 1965

Prelude

Some of my most vivid boyhood memories are of my father's political career. For twenty years he was a North Dakota State Senator, in his last term serving as president of the upper house. This absorbing activity was a hobby. He did not support himself by it. But it was a passionate affair—turbulent, unpredictable, exciting, demanding. And also depressing. I remember what a deep blow it was to him when an appointment to the United States Senate, generally expected to go to him, was at the last minute given to another in payment of an old political debt. He accepted the loss gracefully, though it was a bitter one, because "that's the way politics is."

Winning or losing, through one frenetic campaign after another, he battled with total dedication. He believed in politics—and in politicians. It annoyed him that people thought politics "dirty." To him it was a high calling and he was proud of his political activities and achievements. When I was a boy he would take me out of school to go with him to Bismarck, the state capital, to observe the legislature in session. It was a unique educational experience. I was sharply impressed with the way the legislators would battle on the floor of the House or the Senate and yet remain friends outside. There was mutual respect and *esprit de corps* and in spite of the obvious rough-ness of the game, I could see that these men on the whole trusted one another, both their opponents and their friends. My father rejected the popular image of politicians as pure opportunists and saw instead a surprisingly high ethical stan-dard in the political world. Those who, in his opinion, did not live up to this code earned his lively contempt. And he was not one to hide his feelings in such matters.

So though he made many staunch friends in politics, he also made more than a few enemies. At first it surprised and, I suppose, shocked me to discover the mixed feelings the pub-lic harbors about the officials they elect. As I went about, with some of my schoolmates whom I had corralled, to distribute campaign literature or to procure signatures for various peti-tions, people not knowing my name would express themselves candidly about my father and his political views. It made me angry, of course, if it was unfavorable. But my father took this all in stride and tried to help me see the need for a certain re-silient callousness to survive in political conflict. One had to be sensitive to people, he pointed out, to gain their attention and their support, but one also had to be tough in order to stay in the political game over the long run.

Though my father was a political idealist—in many ways almost an evangelist—he was also solidly pragmatic in his po-litical assessments. One of his basic principles was to count the votes, insofar as they could be determined, *before* the fight. He actually enjoyed a good political no-holds-barred brawl and he was not afraid of losing, but he did not believe in spin-ning the wheels however moral the intent and however sophis-ticated the rationale. Experience had taught him to respect not only the good but the possible and it was this practical view-point that brought him in conflict with some of the ecclesias-tical lobbyists working the legislature. When they appeared before committees which he chaired, he was unfailingly courte-ous, but he was irritated. He resented their attitude of moral superiority toward the political world and especially their as-sumption that every political compromise was *ipso facto* moral betrayal. Furthermore, abstract theological reasoning left him cold. He believed in making things happen and in general he found churchmen lacked know-how in this fundamental political process. I once sent him an abstract ecumenical document on Christian political responsibility. His response was: "So what?" He wanted to hear what could be done. Who was going to make something happen? And how?

With this kind of political indoctrination, it is perhaps not surprising that I look at the church in part from this secular perspective. At first, I did not see the obvious parallels between the political world to which I had been introduced by my father and the ecclesiastical world with which I had identified myself vocationally. Only gradually did I begin to see the church as a political institution. Little by little, largely through unhappy experience, I realized that religious communities had a politics of their own. And the more I saw of it, the more I realized that compared to secular politics, church politics failed more grievously to meet professed standards of human conduct.

I am still not entirely certain why this should be. Perhaps my own experience is exceptional. Or maybe my view is jaundiced. Nevertheless, what I have observed of church politics in local congregations, in denominations, in ecumenical organizations, or in the missionary movement has not impressed me with either its quality or its effectiveness. On the whole, I would say that the church politics I have seen has been bad politics. This is not an invidious moral judgment. I am using "bad" in the sense of something which has gone sour, of something which seems out of joint and not functioning properly, of something which is sick.

Dr. Robert Preus has called my attention to the words of a former Governor of North Dakota, R. A. Nestos, who at a convention of the Synod of the Norwegian Lutheran Church in 1914, in the midst of a bitter fight over whether to merge or not with two other bodies of Norwegian origin, called for the floor and said: "As I have watched the work of the convention, as I have talked with the men who are here in control, as I have noted how domineering the majority is, and how dis-

inclined to treat the minority with even the common cour-
tesies of our business and political life, I am impressed with
the fact that . . . the spirit controlling the proceedings here
would be deplorable even in a political convention and is unworthy of a Synod meeting, where you should have a right to
expect that the Spirit of God would rule both thought and
action. . . ."

Many a case study in church politics has struck me in the
same way. It is not that politics was operating but that, contrary to what one might expect, it seemed to be on a lower
level, seemed to lack some of the élan that makes secular politics viable and, ultimately, even dignified. One of my friends,
church historian E. Clifford Nelson, tells the story of the dead-
locked negotiators in a church merger scheme who were finally locked in a St. Paul, Minnesota, hotel room without a toi-
let and told they wouldn't get out until the agreement came
out first. It did and they were released and relieved. That was
a direct and practical way of solving a political problem, but
somewhat coercive. Still it is not the use of force that corrupts
current church politics. The cause is a less visible virus.

If I were to pinpoint the difference between church and
secular politics, I would say that the former is less honest. It
may seem a paradox to call church politics "dishonest," but
this seems to me the fact of the matter. And perhaps it is not
so difficult to understand. Some explanations for the phenomenon are found in this book; indeed, the book is an attempt
to explain some of these paradoxical elements that church
politics incorporates. To call church politics "dishonest" is
only another way of saying that church politics has tended
to be hidden and camouflaged and thus denied. Modern psychoanalytic insight has helped us to see that such repression
is not only a symptom of sickness but also a cause.

I have taken cases, largely out of the public press, to identify some of the symptoms of the malaise. They come from
Protestant and Catholic quarters. Though each church has
its own political ethos, one of the striking facts about church
politics is its universality. In fact one of the strongest bonds

of ecumenical unity today may be that the churches suffer from the same political ailments. Organizational indigestion and popular alienation are churchly commonplaces—in all sectors of the ecclesiastical world. No one church, no one ecumenical body has a monopoly of malaise in these matters. In church politics we must confess, with Freud, that "we are all sick."

When I was first becoming aware of the political game being played in the churches, especially during my seven years of ecumenical administration in Geneva, I was inclined to blame the persons involved. Many of the ecumenical politicians and their methods appalled me. It was difficult to understand how they could reconcile their obvious drive for power and their ruthless use of it with their Christian piety. Gradually I came to realize that, in many cases, it was not reconciled. They were blissfully unaware of any contradiction between their religious faith and their political life. They were, I finally came to the conclusion, not so much sinister as naive. Some, more candid, rationalized their dubious political maneuvers by the greatness of the "Cause" to which they were ostensibly devoted, but even this divestiture of naïveté does not take the place of real integrity.

The fact was that the whole political situation was unhealthy. It was, as a whole, conducive to bad faith, hypocrisy, and religious schizophrenia. As I have said, I believe now that this condition is largely due to repression. Politics is considered intrinsically bad. Therefore, the politics necessary for organizing, promoting, and developing the life of the church creates deep guilt feelings. The reality of politics and politicians in church life is denied. This hallucinatory gesture does not, of course, do away with church politics but it does deny politics the conditioning and qualifying control which the piety and theology of the Christian community could provide.

The political pathology of church leaders is an unexplored field. My impression of ecclesiastical tycoonery is that the typical church politician is either quite innocent in regard to his own motives, power drives and ambitions, or, insofar as he is aware of the nature of his profession, is deeply ambivalent about his political activities. My father was proud of being a politician. Politics to him was an honorable vocation. It was the science of making desirable things happen in the community. But few church politicians, at least up to now, seem to me to entertain the same high sense of their calling. Such is my conclusion after more than twenty years of observation of the species.

This book is an attempt to bring church politics out into the open, to "tell it like it is," not just to scandalize or to shock, but rather to suggest in a realistic way what the "principalities and powers" are in the organized life of the church, to indicate the political dynamics that are operative in ecclesiastical existence, and to seek to promote an open and healthy church politics which will allow the Christian community to be faithful to the good news it proclaims and relevant to the world where that good news must achieve reality.

I must say a word of acknowledgment and express my appreciation to my wife, Elizabeth, and to Mrs. Glenn R. Parson for their assistance in preparation of the manuscript. Also I would like to thank my students who have patiently suffered through the birth-pangs of many of the ideas here presented. Finally, I would like to mention the names of Philippe Maury and Marvin Halverson, friends now departed, and of William Stringfellow, for aiding by challenge, debate, and consolation in thrashing out some of the basic theses this book propounds.

KEITH R. BRIDSTON

Contents

PRELUDE   7

1-PSYCHEDELICS   15

2-POLITY   40

3-POWER   73

4-PARTICIPATION   106

5-POLITICKING   140

POSTLUDE   163

NOTES   167

1 - *Psychedelics*

There's Nobody Here but Us Christians!

Parishioners Protest Calendar Shift

Storm Rectory, Pummel Priests

By Hugh Hough

A long-simmering dispute over a church calendar turned violent Friday when two priests were attacked by a crowd in the rectory of St. Nicholas Ukrainian Catholic Cathedral after a mass.

During the melee in the rectory, 2243 W. Rice, the Rev. Thomas Glynn was cut and bruised on the face. He was treated at St. Mary of Nazareth Hospital. A second priest, the Rev. William Bilinsky, said he was pinned to the rectory floor by irate parishioners. Four persons, including a physician, were arrested as some 25 policemen quelled the disturbance. The trouble started after an 8 A.M. mass, when churchgoers realized there would be no observance of the Feast of the Epiphany.

No Blessing of Water

As is their custom, members had brought glass jars and little jugs to be filled with water and blessed. But a priest would not perform the rite because of the church calendar change. Friday was Epiphany under the Julian calendar formerly followed by the church. But the Epiphany is celebrated Jan. 6 under the Gregorian calendar—and use of that calendar was decreed in 1964 by the Most Rev. Jaroslav Gabro, bishop of the Ukrainian Catholic Diocese of Chicago. Most Christians use the Gregorian calendar. But traditionalists in the congregation of the large West Side cathedral have continued to press for observances under the Julian calendar.

How It Began

Friday's violence started when a crowd moved from the cathedral across the street to the rectory. Father Bilinsky said protesters surged through the rectory door and, as he phoned the police, he was doused with a pitcher of water. There were conflicting reports of the violence.

Mrs. Ewdokia Onyczkanycz of 2446 W. Iowa said she was hit on the chest by Father Glynn as he sought to stop Roman Dziubynskyj from taking photographs in the rectory. Dziubynskyj, 60, of 2626 W. Walton, whose eyeglasses were smashed during the disturbance, was one of the four persons arrested. He was charged with battery. Others arrested were Teofel Kawka, 63, of 1042 N. Oakley, charged with battery; Suriwka Lubomyr, 42, of 2247 W. Iowa, disorderly conduct and interfering with police, and Dr. P. T. Demus, 51, of 19522 S. Midland, Mokena, the physician, disorderly conduct and resisting arrest.

Father Bilinsky said Dziubynskyj and Kawka, along with members of a committee which he said incited the demonstration, excommunicated themselves by the attack on the priests. Serious infractions of church laws bring this punishment, Father Bilinsky explained. No church action is needed to impose this punishment, he said; the persons in effect impose it on themselves.

What It Means

Excommunication means a person is barred from all church sacraments except confession, until absolved.

Father Bilinsky said the excommunication applies to members of the Committee for the Defense of the Traditions of the Ukrainian Catholic Church. The priest said the committee passed out leaflets last Sunday inciting the demonstration on Friday. The church's excommunication laws were explained by Bishop Gabro, after a similar demonstration at the church August 28. During that melee, a group broke into the rectory office and attacked Msgr. Peter Leskiw, the church's pastor. He suffered face and scalp cuts and bruises in the incident. Several persons excommunicated themselves because of that action, Bishop Gabro said.

After the rectory disturbance Friday, police tried to break up a crowd of 200 persons outside. Some threw snowballs at the rectory door and there were scuffles with policemen and shouts of "police brutality." As policemen moved the crowd back, Dr. Demus fell to the ground and then was taken to a police wagon. A policeman charged the doctor had bitten him.

In the group were many middle-aged women, a number of them wearing head scarves. Many members of the church are emigrants from Eastern Europe. One woman said: "We just wanted him (the priest) to bless the water. We ask and they call police. I feel very bad. In Russia, my mother gets water blessed, and I'm here in a free country and I can't."

Another woman, who said she was a long-time member, declared: "My parents 53 years ago were building this church, and now we cannot come and worship as we wish. Are we not Christians?"

Said a man nearby: "These are the people who escaped communism. They want only to come to church and pray."[1]

Church politics appears to be confusing only because it is. The case of the Ukrainian Catholic parish in Chicago vividly illustrates the kaleidoscopic variety of patterns and dynamics which the organized life of the Christian community presents. There are not only images projected on a flat plane. The life of the church—indeed of any religious association—is multidimensional. One may view it from a number of different perspectives, and each illuminates the subject in a different way. And that, in part, creates the problem. Which viewpoint is most accurate? Which provides the most adequate explanation of the phenomena? Which offers the most comprehensive depiction of the church's existence?

The traditional assumption is that the church is unique. It is a special entity, a wonderful and sacred mystery, which defies ordinary analysis. It is a "peculiar" institution. It is described and defined in terms of its own peculiar science—theology. It has its own peculiar story—church history. It has its own peculiar structure—Christ's Body. It exists and operates according to its own peculiar dogmatic constitution. It has its own peculiar behavior—a spiritual life. It has its own peculiar sustenance—heavenly food and drink. It is, in a peculiar way, a city of God on earth. And its inhabitants are peculiar strangers and pilgrims in this world. This is the commonly accepted concept of the church's character.

How is one then to explain the fact that the life and thought and action of this "peculiar" body is so similar to other organizations and associations and institutions? Its intellectual life may be considered a product of revelation, but its theology has many familiar marks of man's philosophical reflection and rational enterprise. Its history intersects with secular history. Its structure bears the ordinary sociological marks of other institutions. Its constitution is not unlike those of earthly corporations. Its behavior and activity psychologically parallel those of other individuals and groups. As a "city of God" its structures show a suspicious cartographic resemblance to earthly counterparts. Is the church then, as a social institution, strange? Yes. Peculiar? Yes. Unique? No. The church is in part a creation of man—a product of his worldly as well as his spiritual experiences—and as such bears resemblance to other human institutions.

Church politics? At Vatican Council II reporters and journalists from the secular press recorded some of the proceedings in regular secular political terminology. They spoke of liberal and conservative groups, blocs of delegates, majority and minority votes, ballots, caucuses, power-plays, maneuvers, domination, factions. Eventually a spokesman of the Vatican reprimanded them. This was not, he explained, a political meeting and it was inappropriate to use political terms to describe what they were observing. But what were they observing? If it was not politics, what was it? Was it only an apparent similarity? Did it only *seem* to be like other political conventions and assemblies they had observed? Just how "peculiar" was Vatican II politically speaking? How different from secular convocations?

The Dogmatic Constitution on the Church of Vatican II, in the section "The Call of the Whole Church to Holiness," asserts: "Faith teaches that the Church, whose mystery is being set forth by this sacred Synod, is holy in a way which can never fail. . . . Now, this holiness of the Church is unceasingly manifested, as it ought to be, through those fruits of grace that the Spirit produces in the faithful. . . . All of Christ's faithful, therefore, whatever be the conditions, duties, and circumstances of their lives, will grow in holiness day by day through these very situations. . . ."[2] But what about parishioners pummeling priests? Is that part of being "holy in a way which can never fail"? Is this a mysterious and peculiar example of the "holiness of the Church . . . unceasingly manifested"? Is this the peculiar way in which the faithful "will grow in holiness day by day"?

Presumably the theological answer to this paradoxical phenomenon is found in the same document: "Christ, the one Mediator, established and ceaselessly sustains here on earth His holy Church, the community of faith, hope, and charity, as a visible structure. Through her He communicates truth and grace to all. But the society furnished with hierarchical agencies and the Mystical Body of Christ are not to be considered as two realities, nor are the visible assembly and the spiritual community, nor the earthly Church and the Church enriched with heavenly things. Rather they form one interlocked reality which comprises a divine and a human element. For this reason, by an excellent analogy, this reality is compared to the mystery of the Incarnate Word."

Perhaps in anticipation of the impious thoughts passing through the mind of priests pinned to the floor by irate parishioners, all too aware of the "interlocked reality which comprises a divine and a human element," the document goes on to admit that "on this earth the Church is marked by a genuine though imperfect holiness." That is, "until there is a new heaven and a new earth where justice dwells (cf. 2 Pet. 3:13), the pilgrim Church in her sacraments and institutions, which pertain to this present time, takes on the appearance of this passing world. She herself dwells among creatures who groan and travail in pain and await the revelation of the sons of God (cf. Rom. 8:19-22)."[3]

These lofty theological pronouncements were probably of dubious comfort to the water-soaked and battered priests in St. Nicholas Ukrainian Catholic Cathedral in Chicago, who probably found their Bibles of more immediate use as instruments of defense than as source books to confirm theologians' theories. Even though the attacked priest might have identified himself as one of the "creatures who groan and travail in pain" and "await the revelation of the sons of God," the "appearance of this passing world" in the form of policemen was probably more reassuring to him as he faced the outraged Ukrainian housewives than lofty visions of "The Eschatological Nature of the Pilgrim Church and Her Union with the Heavenly Church."

The Case of the Parishioners' Protest exhibits the complexities of interpreting the life of the church. Admittedly a bizarre, perhaps a caricatured example, it nevertheless illustrates the difficulty of correlating the theological self-image of the church with its external appearance. As the "long-time member" plaintively asks: "Are we not Christians?" Yes. And more.

For example, the historian would point out that the difference in dating Epiphany in the church calendar arises from a division between the Eastern and Western Catholic traditions. And this split might be explained in terms of intellectual, cultural, ethnic, or sociological factors, which are all part of the story of the break between Byzantine and Roman Christianity. The fact that this ancient bifurcation erupts in Chicago, the most authentically American of the cities of the New World, hundreds of years and thousands of miles away, exhibits the "eternal" attributes of the church in a somewhat different light than the ordinary theological significance of that term might connote.

Or the sociologist would note that many members of the church involved are emigrants from Eastern Europe. It would suggest to him that this church is not simply an association of those with a common faith or identical doctrinal convictions but an institutional extension of an ethnic community. He might also assume that the religious institution provides the major symbol for the ethnic and cultural identity of its uprooted members. In a strange and foreign land they look to the church as the conservator of the familiar customs and traditions of their native country. It is to them both a symbol and a guarantee of their cultural inheritance. H. Richard Niebuhr, in his pioneering study *Social Sources of Denominationalism,* has chronicled this interplay of sociological and theological factors in the development of the institutional configuration of American Christianity. The church, he concluded, inevitably fulfills many functions beyond its strictly religious and liturgical purposes. A later book of Niebuhr's, *Christ and Culture,* outlines the various answers that have been given in Christian history as to the appropriateness or inappropriateness of this connection and the differences between individual thinkers and theological traditions on the proper limits of this interlocking of the secular and religious dimensions of the church's existence. Whatever position is held—whether outright rejection or complete acquiescence—it is evident that the problem of the right relation between the church as a spiritual body and the church as a sociological community does not lend itself to simplistic resolution.

Karl Rahner, the Austrian Jesuit theologian, argues this persuasively in his essay "Christians in the Modern World." Pointing out the fallacies in the "ghetto idea" of the church, he says: "The ghetto policy consists of thinking of the Church not only as the autonomous community of salvation (which she is) but as an autonomous society in every field. . . . The interior structure of the ghetto conforms, inevitably, to the style of that period which it is, in make-believe, preserving; its human types are those sociological, intellectual and cultural types which belong to that period and feel comfortable in the ghetto." This confusion arises, Rahner believes, from a fundamental "ontological heresy" which denies a necessary dialectic to the relation of church and world: "In the sphere of secular, worldly living, there is never any period that can be called *the* Christian culture, etc. This does not only mean that according to Catholic teaching there are always Church and State, redemptive history and secular history, nature and grace, and that these can never be adequately united in one thing. It means, rather, that it is never possible simply to deduce, from Christian principles of belief and morality, any one single pattern of the world as it ought to be. In principle, there is neither in respect of the State nor of economics nor of culture nor of history, any one clear, concrete imperative which can be deduced from Christian teaching as the one and only possible right course. . . . there can never (apart from the Church herself) be any single concrete thing in the sphere of world history and culture which can lay claim to be, in principle, uniquely and exclusively *the* Christian realization of anything." Thus, Rahner continues, it is illegitimate to identify any particular historical manifestation of the Christian spirit with the ultimate principles themselves, as, for instance, when we speak of the *Christian* Middle Ages and identify Western civilization with Christianity. The fact is, he says, that such embodiments, impressive as they may be, come about "not because of Christian principles but because of geographical, technical, economic and other factors; so that *at that time* any general desire to exist in a Christian fashion was probably almost bound to produce what in fact was then produced."[4]

From this theological perspective it is entirely justifiable, even necessary, to use the various insights of the social sciences to analyze church history as well as present church life. For example, as Rahner suggests, "the value set upon the Church in public life, in its medieval form, is not attributable, as a phenomenon, simply and solely to the supernatural power of the Church and Christianity. That particular form (not the Church's essential theological value) was also, at least in its factual existential realization, the result of temporal, secular combinations of historical forces. It was a fact of cultural history rather than of theology. One might say that every 'Middle Ages' (i.e., every culture resting on a peasant and small-city foundation, and remaining historically stationary for a whole period) has its ruling religion, established in unchallenged supremacy; this without reference to whether such religion be true or false, from below or from above, medieval Islam, or medieval feudal Shintoism in Japan, or anything else."[5]

Such an acknowledgment that Christianity "like other cultural religions, did in one particular, necessarily passing, stage of that culture, exercise a practically unchallenged ruling power over the hearts of men and their cultural institutions," but that it will continue to manifest itself in other forms and fashions in terms of cultural synthesis at other stages, opens the door to a wide range of interpretations of the church's existence and its history. And it would also suggest that in spite of still remaining ecclesiological differences over the significance and content of the "Christian essence" or the "Church's essential theological value," there is a growing ecumenical consensus between Protestant and Catholic scholars on the need of a multidisciplinary approach for the analysis of Christian phenomena.

To return to the Chicago case, and reflect on it in the frame of reference of another discipline—cultural anthropology—we find clues in the behavior of the participants which, from a purely religious standpoint, seem to be irrational and reprehensible, but from an anthropologist's perspective, are not only scientifically identifiable but even sympathetically understandable. The significance attached to the blessing of the water at a particular time and under certain ritualized circumstances appears on the face of it to be out of all proportion to its intrinsic importance, certainly in terms of the ultimate purpose of the church. But here we must come to terms with the factor of magic in religious life. Theoretically, and referring to dogmatic criteria, magic is denied legitimacy in the church. Yet, according to Sir James Frazer, the public profession of magic has helped to release men from their bondage to tradition into a newer and broader world outlook. A great service has thus been rendered to humanity. Many would agree with the conclusion of Sir James: "When we remember further that in another direction magic has paved the way for science, we are forced to admit that if the black art has done much evil, it has also been the source of much good; that if it is the child of error, it has yet been the mother of freedom and truth."[6]

Recent cultural anthropologists have identified the residual benefits of magic in specific terms. Positive functions of magic are recognized as beneficial in certain groups and cultures. The test of the benefits is wholly pragmatic. Standard formularies of spell, rite, and taboo have been utilized for long periods of time without the slightest deviation. The continuation of magic in any culture affirms a measure of confidence in the rite. Here is a belief that satisfies. It works the spell of control and mastery over outside forces.

Professor E. O. James accents this viewpoint in his Public Lectures at Oxford (1932) in these terms: "Today, it is true, a scientific apologetic is becoming established which is calculated to give a new lease of life to all that is most vital in the ancient faith and practice of Christendom, but it behoves theologians who are engaged in the re-statement of traditional Christianity in terms of modern knowledge, to bear in mind the cultural significance of the sacred mythology which lives in our ritual, in our morality, and hitherto has governed our faith and controlled our conduct."[7]

Thus a shift in the date of the observance of Epiphany is, from this viewpoint, a most significant one and with far more profound repercussions entailed than a simple commonsense reading of the data would foresee. Furthermore, the anthropologist might be willing to grant to this magical expectancy a certain rational confirmation that a purely dogmatic perspective almost inevitably rejects.

In other words, we have the ironical situation in which the church, attempting to modernize itself and become up to date, reforms its anachronistic patterns of ritual action and finds itself abandoning what the modern anthropologist accepts as pragmatically effective!

The matter does not rest here. Bronislaw Malinowski wonders whether this kind of magical dynamic might not be transposed and transformed and integrated in terms of a constructive faith. Or, to put it another way, can primitive magic be transfigured into civilization? The delicate dilemma which presents itself is this: Can a social structure be realized which embodies the principles of love, justice, and freedom? Is there a social reality for faith? For, as Malinowski admits (particularly as the modern experience with totalitarianism reveals), "You can translate the constructive drives" of man in an effort to achieve civilization in such a way that "the very fountainheads of creative and constructive work are killed."[8]

In short, the potent, magically invoked drives of man may be harnessed in a rational, scientific system for demonic ends. The church as a human institution is no more immune from this possibility than any other social structure, and indeed may be more susceptible because of superstitious assumptions about its nature and purpose. Reinhold Niebuhr, writing of cases in which the church itself has become tyrannical, describes the source of error as the use of religion's force "to increase rather than to mitigate the natural self-deception and pretension of the human heart. . . . It is because religion may issue in either a contrite subjection of all human ideals to the holiness of God or in a false identification of those ideals with the divine perfection that it is impossible to regard any religion as good *per se*. The final and most sinful pretension of the human spirit is always expressed religiously."[9]

The history of religions offers some interesting examples of the struggle to make such distinctions as differentiate the concept of taboo and the idea of holiness. In many primitive cultures the two are practically identical, as are magic and religion. In fact, the term "taboo" is taken from Polynesian usage in which the word represents the whole religious system. But it appears to be a general phenomenon. W. Robertson-Smith and other experts in Semitic religions have shown how the rules of holiness are related to savage taboos concerning purity and impurity, cleanness and uncleanness, in a physical sense—dietary, sexual, and burial observances, for instance. There are common roots, but there is a point at which holiness becomes differentiated from taboo. In Judaism, the idea of purity is elevated to a moral principle, a matter of the heart and spirit, a question of motivation and intent. It is no longer simply identified with physical elements, its observance based on the fear of bodily danger, its character entirely negative, its system altogether illogical, and its enforcement irrational, as in the case of taboo. As Ernst Cassirer in *An Essay on Man* indicates in his discussion of this evolution, magic in this and other forms never completely gives way its ground to religion, as is the thesis of Sir James Frazer. Rather, religious evolution is a much more complicated, a much slower process: "It does not mean the complete destruction of the first and fundamental mental characteristics of mythical thought. . . . The prophets predicted a new heaven and a new earth. What is really new is not the contents of this prophetic religion but its inner tendency, its ethical meaning. One of the greatest miracles that all the higher religions had to perform was to develop their new character, their ethical and religious interpretation of life, out of the crude raw material of the most primitive conceptions, the grossest superstitions. . . . All the higher ethical religions—the religion of the prophets of Israel, Zoroastrianism, Christianity—set themselves a common task. They relieve the intolerable burden of the taboo system; but they detect, on the other hand, a more profound sense of religious obligation that instead of being a restriction or compulsion is the expression of a new positive ideal of human freedom."[10]

A similar differential evolution is seen in regard to the sacraments in the Christian tradition. Few topics have vexed the church so much, or have been the cause of such acrimonious debate in church history. Again, the reason—against the background just sketched—is not difficult to appreciate. That the uproar in the Chicago church was sparked by a question of sacramental observance was almost predictable, whatever other factors of unrest and disquiet may have been involved. Oliver Quick, in his study *The Christian Sacraments,* expounds the difficulty in differentiating between crude and magical ideas and symbolic and mystical conceptions of Real Presence. In his analysis of the doctrine of transubstantiation he shows the strenuous efforts of St. Thomas Aquinas to go beyond the simple, materialistic views of presence to a much more sophisticated and scientifically rational position, without in the process destroying the "fountainheads" of liturgical devotion. That popular piety and "folk-theology" conceptions have not been able entirely to digest that intellectual transformation is perhaps indicated by the tendency of some Catholic theologians today to abandon the term "transubstantiation" entirely and substitute ones such as "transvaluation," which do not seem to carry such a heavy weight of magical connotations.

In any case, it is evident that what the church formally defines and teaches (the Council of Trent established the position of Aquinas on transubstantiation as normative) is no guarantee that cruder, more primitive conceptions will not continue to be operative in the constituency at a popular level. Whatever the church theologians and authorities may have intended by the rite of blessing the water at Epiphany, or may themselves have understood by it, the actual reception of the rite may be taking place on a different conceptual level and within a different religious context.

This brings us, finally, to a psychological view of the scene. These disparities and contradictions between formal, ecclesiastical theology and operative "folk" theology, between external manifestation and internal cause, between the meaning intended and the meaning received, between confessed creed and actual belief, are, in part at least, symptomatic of what Freud was dealing with in *The Psychopathology of Every-day Life*. It is now a commonplace that every psychological symp-tom has a psychological cause and that the cause is often at the subconscious level, repressed and thus unknown to the patient. Furthermore, largely through the insight of Freud, we have been made aware that "hallucinations and delusions are not at all meaningless or irrational, that they have their *raison d'être*. In no light sense may we say that there is method in madness."[11]

The Chicago case as reported makes clear certain reasons for the melee, but the evidence does not fully illuminate the basic cause or causes of the "madness." The brute passions aroused, the irrational fury of the parishioners, are not fully explicated by the external facts of the case. The actions of those who threw snowballs at the rectory door, engaged them-selves in scuffles with policemen, broke into the rectory of-fice and attacked the church's pastor, and doused another priest with a pitcher of water hardly seem to be consonant with the spirit of a group who had "only come to church to pray." The doctor charged with biting a policeman seems to conform neither to the ordinary religious image of the devout layman nor to the professional image of a physician aware of the unhygienic implications of such an action.

Such hysterical phenomena, however, from the psycho-analytic point of view are neither strange nor peculiar. The aggressive component in human personality often finds dif-ficulty in expression in sophisticated, polite society. Men have had to seek for suitable outlets. Wit, for example, can become a socially acceptable way to express hostility and aggression without incurring disapproval or ostracism. Here again the idea that "psychological energy has the property of being dis-placeable" is a fundamental principle in psychoanalytic theory and practice. This happens by "a series of energy displacements or object substitutions. The source and aim of the instinct remain the same when energy is displaced; it is only the goal object that varies. . . . The causes of displacement are the same as those that produce all personality development, namely maturation, frustration, conflict, inadequacy, and anxiety."[12]

One of the classic examples of this is found in what is called "oral gratification." Eating and sucking represent satisfaction both through meeting the demands of hunger and the gratifications of pleasurable stimulation: "As he grows older, childish forms of lip stimulation are abandoned under social pressure and adult ways are adopted. Smoking, kissing, wetting the lips with the tongue, applying lipstick, drinking, whistling, singing, talking, chewing gum and tobacco, and spitting are some of the oral activities engaged in by adults." This substitutionary rechanneling of instinctual energies does not mean a simple displacement for the adult as it does for the child. For the former, it is characteristic that such object-choices "are determined by a confluence of energy from many vital sources. This is known as the *fusion of instincts.* Adult interests and preferences, unlike those of children, are complexly motivated, or as Freud expressed it, they are *overdetermined.* By overdetermination is meant that any given object-choice might satisfy a multiplicity of instincts."[13] Such "condensations"—kissing is both orally stimulating and sexually gratifying, to take a simple example—are not easy to break down into their multimotivated components. Thus the incident of the doctor biting the policeman probably cannot be adequately explained simply in terms of the "angry medical man."

In fact, biting has very definite psychodynamic overtones. It is obviously an aggressive, if not hostile, action. At the same time, it is related to the area of oral gratification already mentioned. It may be instructive to note in this connection that the original Greek text for the words of institution of the Eucharist could be translated: "Take, *bite,* this is my body. . . ." Thus, the elements of aggression *and* gratification are fused in a single symbolic activity, religiously sanctioned and ceremonially celebrated. This is what the psychoanalytic observer would call sublimation: "When the substitute object is one that represents a higher cultural goal, this type of displacement is called a *sublimation.* Examples of sublimation are the deflection of energy into intellectual, humanitarian, cultural, and artistic pursuits. Freud points out that the development of civilization is made possible by the inhibition of primitive object-cathexes. The energy which is prevented from discharging itself in direct ways is diverted into socially useful and culturally creative channels. Sublimation does not result in complete satisfaction; there is always some residual tension which cannot be discharged by sublimated object-choices. This tension is responsible, in part, for the nervousness of civilized man, but it is also responsible for the highest achievements of mankind."[14]

Excommunication, or the threat of excommunication, could be seen then as the withdrawal of the sublimated object of gratification and aggression. This, in effect, forces a return to a more crude form of displacement; eating the sacramental bread is replaced by biting the policeman! Or, to interpret this phenomenon in terms of the group, their wants and wishes (i.e., "We just *wanted* him to bless the water," "now we cannot come and worship as we *wish,*" "they *want* only to come to church and pray") are denied fulfillment and ritual confirmation by the change in the church calendar. Blocked by the hierarchical authorities, they then form a "Committee for the Defense of the Traditions of the Ukrainian Catholic Church." When they are blocked again by clerical authority, this time reinforced by civil power, there is a chaotic eruption of violence on the part of the members. Thus the "demonstration" on January 19, as well as the one on the previous August 28, becomes a symbol not only of direct confrontation but of a far more profound psychological and spiritual malaise in the church's communal existence.

All this is the raw material of church politics. Politics is defined as the science and art of government. It has also been said that "the name of the game is power." In either case, the term is neutral. There can be good and bad politics, just as there can be good or bad government. Political science, as an academic discipline, is concerned with the study and analysis of political structures and processes, forms and dynamics, in the distribution and ordering of political life. On the scientific side, the Chicago case appears to be an example of dysfunctionalism, of a breakdown in the formal political processes of an institution. The hierarchical authority has "decreed" the use of the Gregorian calendar. The clerical subordinates execute the decision. But the constituency, at least part of it, refuses to accede. There is resistance and finally rebellion by the governed. There is a development of counterorganization—the "Committee"—which challenges the established powers. The unresolved conflict of these powers gradually deteriorates into open violence—a formal rupture of constitutional relationships (i.e., "excommunication" and disobedience) and a beginning of overt warfare. The political problem is then to analyze the sources of the political dysfunctioning and suggest new institutional forms and processes to correct the ills. In other words, a new policy and a new program have to be formulated to re-establish political harmony and social equilibrium.

It is precisely here, of course, that the understanding of politics as the *art* of government is so important. Political reform, the restricted sense of restructuring the institution or modifying the political processes to make them more rational and functional, may be only a formal attempt to alleviate the symptoms. But the fundamental causes of the illness may be left untouched. Manipulation is not unfamiliar as a political technique but it very seldom, if ever, does more than delay political dissolution and often, if not always, only aggravates the basic political ills of a system and makes its overthrow that much more violent in the final analysis.

The science *and* art of politics is, therefore, not only a technical understanding of the political scene but also a certain intuitive insight into its inner meaning which transcends a pure rational, "scientific" appraisal of the external topography and the formal events. From the scientific side, the politician must be fully cognizant of the political apparatus itself. A novel such as *Advise and Consent* shows how difficult this can be if the political structure is highly complex and sophisticated. Even very skilled and well-experienced professionals can be outwitted by it and, indeed, part of the political game is to play upon the ignorance, stupidity, or negligence of one's opponents in this regard. Certainly history shows that few political leaders have achieved eminence, or remained in power long, who have not had this scientific awareness of the system in which they were operating.

Along with this technical proficiency in respect to the political structures and processes themselves, the professional politician requires scientific appreciation of the powers and forces that provide the dynamic of political life. This power complex, as has been indicated, is made up of historical, ethnic, magical, psychological, and other forces which are at the same time distinguishable and yet politically inextricably bound up with one another. The dramatic, almost terrifying, concentration of this power into a vote—the casting of this power one way or another on a particular issue or in favor of one candidate over against another—is part of the frustration inherent in politics. Yet, at the same time, this radical simplification and focusing of the power complex is what gives politics its fascination, as well as that which purifies it and redeems it from theoretical abstraction and analytic paralysis. The politician knows—not entirely and not always, of course—where his power comes from, why certain individuals or particular groups give him support or withhold it. His platform, the style of his campaign, the character of his speeches, as well as the votes he casts once in office, all reflect his assessment of these power factors. Jay Gould, the American industrial baron, asked by a legislative committee: "What are your politics, Mr. Gould?" replied with cynical candor: "Well, in a Republican district I am Republican, in a Democratic district I am Democrat; but I am always an Erie Railroad man." No politician, however assiduously he might avoid that kind of candid disclosure, is unaware of the force of the statement or does not to some extent live by that principle. It is, to use the familiar aphorism, knowing on which side one's bread is buttered.

In the broadest sense, this is what political economy means. Plato's argument in *The Republic* is in some measure posited on this premise that government ought to be based on science. That is, the philosopher should be the ruler because he has the insight and understanding to constitute and maintain a truly just human state. In his "Seventh Letter," Plato, then an old man, referred to the views he held as a youth in his twenties. He wrote: "Law and morality were deteriorating at an alarming rate, with the result that though I had been full of eagerness for a political career, the sight of all this chaos made me giddy, and though I never stopped thinking how things might be improved and the constitution reformed, I postponed action, waiting for a favorable opportunity. Finally I came to the conclusion that all existing states were incapable of reform without drastic treatment and a great deal of good luck. I was forced, in fact, to the belief that the only hope of finding justice for society or for the individual lay in true philosophy, and that mankind will have no respite from trouble until either real philosophers gain political power or politicians become by some miracle philosophers."[15]

George Bernard Shaw argues in the *Fabian Essays* that political economy was forced into existence by the increasing complexities of political life provoked by industrial society. The Middle Ages, he says, had a simplicity which lent itself to simple political structures and procedures. But this is no longer the situation: "This Social Order, relics of which are still to be found in all directions, did not collapse because it was unjust or absurd. It was burst by the growth of the social organism. Its machinery was too primitive, and its administration too naive, too personal, too meddlesome to cope with anything more complex than a group of industrially independent communes, centralized very loosely, if at all, for purely political purposes. . . . The desperate effort of the human intellect to unravel this tangle of industrial anarchy brought modern political economy into existence."[16]

But even taking that into consideration, and recognizing the increasing complexity of modern society, certainly Plato's conviction of the need for wisdom and expertise in the political enterprise is not foreign to Shaw's analysis, nor are their conclusions dissimilar. They are both convinced that political health is to some extent dependent on the scientific sophistication and the rational capabilities of the political participants, especially the leaders. However, Plato's reference to the factor of "good luck," and the very term "philosopher" itself, hints at an element of transcendent unpredictability and mystery in the political sphere which is not entirely reducible to rational, scientific categories. In doing so, he appears to be approaching the view that politics is an "art," not merely a "science."

It is probably a precarious thing to try to identify this elusive dimension in politics, or the "artistic" quality and capacity in politicians. Nevertheless, there is no doubt that it is a crucial element in political existence. C. P. Snow in *Variety of Men,* a "set of personal impressions" of men who have affected the shape and spirit of the twentieth century, speaks of a perhaps analogous phenomenon when he distinguishes "judgment" and "insight" in his chapter on Winston Churchill: "Judgment, to people concerned with political decisions, means two things—one which most of us would think good, one bad. The bad thing is the ability to guess what everyone else is thinking, and think like them. This Churchill never had, and would have despised himself for having. But the good thing in 'judgment' is the ability to think of many matters at once, of their interdependence, their relative importance, and their consequences." It is Snow's opinion that in many ways, and on many occasions, Churchill's judgment was "seriously defective." "Yet," he goes on, "ironically this same obsessive quality, which often distorted his judgment and led him into errors, was also the force which drove him into the cardinal achievement of his life. Judgment is a fine thing: but it is not all that uncommon. Deep insight is much rarer. Churchill had flashes of that kind of insight, dug up from his own nature, independent of influences, owing nothing to anyone outside himself. Sometimes it was a better guide than judgment; in the ultimate crisis when he came to power, there were times when judgment itself could, though it did not need to, become a source of weakness."[17] In this light, the fact that Churchill's hobby was painting may be taken as having more than ordinary significance.

Closely related to insight as an artistic virtue is vision. Insight might be considered that ability of an artist to have a depth awareness and appreciation of what is. Vision might be considered the ability to see what ought to be. Insight without vision can lead to cynicism and despair. Vision without insight can lead to hallucination and utopianism. Politically translated, this means that pure insight can become the basis for cold calculation, sheer opportunism, without any redeeming qualities furnished by a transcendent image of what ought to or might be. And it also means that pure vision can become the basis for wild fantasy, disengaged dream worlds, without the sobering qualifications imposed by a realistic recognition of what is and has been. Karl Mannheim's *Ideology and Utopia* is one among many studies which illustrate with historical examples the distortions and fallacies which are developed out of such kinds of one-sidedness.

Another ecclesiastical case, also somewhat bizarre and melodramatic but coming from a completely different side of the church spectrum and out of a radically different context than that of the Ukrainian Cathedral, may illustrate the phenomenon in church politics:

Congregation Beat Him, Declares Minister

BLYTHEVILLE, Ark. (UPI)—The Rev. Edward R. Black said he had just ended his final sermon at the New Providence Baptist Church when his congregation fell upon him and beat him full sore.

The trouble was, according to a deacon, the Baptist preacher offered up a mighty plea unto the Lord to "strike 'em all dead."

This left the flock so wroth, said Deacon Charles Buck, that ladies even rent each others' raiments.

Preacher Black said he turned the other cheek, only to have a lady poke him in the eye with her crutch. As a matter of fact, said Preacher Black, "I don't know how I got out of there. They probably didn't want a murder rap."

The action, it was revealed in municipal court here Wednesday, took place Sunday in the 160-member church at Buckeye. Black said he had resigned as pastor and had preached his final sermon. Deacon Buck said church members had voted last month to remove the board of deacons from office.

Buck said he arose after the sermon to make an announcement, and that's when the Sabbath started getting violated.

"The preacher refused to let the announcement be made," he said. "That started an argument between the pastor and some other men. The preacher ordered them out of the house.

"Then," Buck continued, "he prayed this unusual prayer."

According to the deacon, it was unusual in that Preacher Black urged the Lord to strike the congregation dead.

Black said he wasn't certain about that. "I prayed to strike them to keep them from preventing the worship service."

Some of the ladies of the church, sore grieved over the matter, "got into a little hairpulling combat in the vestibule," Buck said. "After the women got into the battle, that sparked a fight between some men."

"For the Lord's sake, stop!" cried Preacher Black to his erring flock, which was evidently not the right thing to say at the time.

For, Black related, somebody clouted him "with such force that they tell me my glasses flew from the foyer two rows into the church.

"Two women hit me. One woman hit me in the eye with her crutch. Then they all began to hit me.

"I thought they were going to kill me. I was lying on the floor and three of them were stomping me with their feet."

Black hailed Buck and several other members of the congregation before Judge Graham Sudbury on disturbing the peace charges, and the hearing was recessed until next week. Black said he has double vision and possible sight impairment in his left eye, two fractures of his right hand and must undergo an operation Friday as a result of Sunday's service.[18]

The case exhibits many defects not only in political science but in political art. Granted that the report might be inadequate and the account incomplete, nevertheless, with all its extravagant and bizarre features, the incident does ring true as an example of church politics. The forces at work, as in the case of the Ukrainian congregation, are more nakedly exposed than in most instances. Not every church service results in disturbing-the-peace charges. Not every Sunday worship leads to the Sabbath being violated. And in many churches there may be murder in the parishioners' hearts as a result of their ministers' prayers and sermons, but it is seldom that these feelings get expressed in beating, stomping, gouging, and clouting. Not all congregational political struggles end up in municipal court.

But is this case really so peculiar? If it is somewhat demythologized and the essential elements projected into other, perhaps more sedate and conventional settings, there are few ministers or members who cannot identify with it. Without much difficulty, they could provide their own analogous cases out of their experience of church life: tensions, conflicts, pettiness, jealousies, resentments, hostilities, aggravations, hurts, misunderstandings, divisions. As his epistles to the Corinthian church and to other churches amply testify, St. Paul was well aware of this. Yet, and this may be his measure both as a theologian and a church politician, Paul saw much more than this. He had insight, but he also had vision. He was an artist. He saw and he wrote. On one hand, he observed dissensions, quarreling, foolishness, weakness, jealousy, strife, arrogance, immorality; he was conscious that he was addressing those who had been the immoral, the idolaters, the adulterers, the perverts, the thieves, the grabbers, the drunkards, the slanderers, the swindlers. His insight made him all too aware of the earth in the treasured vessels. Yet he was also aware that it is just such a body that is a "temple of the Holy Spirit within" and that, though it is possible and all too easy to do the opposite, there is the potentiality to "glorify God in your body." Despite all the contradictions, in his vision of this strange, bizarre, twisted, and tormented association he saw a brotherhood—in fact, the Body of Christ.

So he added to insight, vision; and to vision, imagination. This imaginative translation of the realities unveiled by insight into the plastic vision of man's true being and destiny is the crux of the art of politics. What so often happens in church politics, whether in the Ukrainian Catholic Cathedral in Chicago or the New Providence Baptist Church in Arkansas, is that judgment, insight, and vision cannot be imaginatively conjoined in the understanding of the church and in the participation in its life. The unusual prayer leads to violence and disruption, the invocation of the name of the Lord leads to assault and battery. The whole affair leads to "double vision." But that is precisely what was needed in the first place though of another sort.

This imaginative capacity—the ability to see the visible association or institution in terms of its essential nature, its peculiar spirit, its ultimate purpose, its special destiny—is the highest level of the science of government and the art of politics. Without it, the people perish. Herbert Read writes of the profound interrelation of the artist and the community in creative work. It seems to involve a contradiction. But, ultimately, says Read, it does not: "The paradox can only be explained metaphysically. The ultimate values of art transcend the individual and his time and circumstances. They express an ideal proportion of harmony which the artist can grasp only by virtue of his intuitive powers. In expressing his intuition the artist will use materials placed in his hands by the circumstances of his time: at one period he will scratch on the walls of his cave, at another he will build or decorate a temple or a cathedral, at another time he will paint on canvas for a limited circle of connoisseurs. The true artist is indifferent to the materials and conditions imposed upon him. He accepts any conditions, so long as they can be used to express his will-to-form. Then in the wider mutations of history his efforts are magnified or diminished, taken up or dismissed, by forces which he cannot predict, and which have very little to do with the values of which he is the exponent. It is his faith that those values are nevertheless among the eternal attributes of humanity."[19]

One of the most persistent images in the Bible is that of God as the artist—the architect, the potter, the creator. And it is from this primal image that St. Paul derives his own political self-image—the "skilled master builder." In so doing, he may be providing an archetypal model of the church politician, as well as a new perspective on the nature and purpose of church politics.

2-*Polity*

Something Funny Happened on the Way to the Form

Mae West Raps Modern Bedtime Movies

HOLLYWOOD—(NEA)—In most people's minds, Mae West and sex go together like apple pie and vanilla ice cream. And you might expect her to be all in favor of today's anything-goes movies.

She isn't.

Mae sat in her living room, all white and gold and mirrored and adorned with cupids and nude statues and paintings and she primly clutched a long, pale-green wraparound robe about her. She's rumored to be in her mid-70s, but her hair is still platinum and there aren't too many wrinkles noticeable and her figure is still an hour glass on daylight saving time.

"My old movies," she said, "used to be thought of as pretty racy. I did a lot with movement—like this and like that—all very animated, you know. Lots of animation. But there was never anything indecent in them.

"Why, I don't think I ever even kissed anybody. I'd get close, but never kiss."

She clutched the robe tighter around her legs.

"But nowadays," she said, "all this bed stuff in pictures. I suppose it's all right if the people are attractive, but too many of the girls are skinny. They have nothing up here, and who wants to see them?

"I guess I'm a bit straitlaced, but I think they go too far these days. They should leave some things to the imagination. I think the imagination is sexier than when everything is obvious, don't you?"

Mae went on to discuss her strait-lacedness.

"I don't swear," she said, "and I don't like to hear swearing. I don't tell dirty jokes and I don't like to hear them told in my presence. There were thousands of dirty jokes made up about me—some of them were kind of funny—but I didn't like to hear them."

Mae West hasn't been too active in the last few years, but not through any lack of interest on the part of producers.[1]

Pope Urges Faith in Church Dogma

VATICAN CITY.

Pope Paul VI, in his papacy's most sweeping pronouncement on faith, appealed to Roman Catholics last night to hold to church dogma on points from papal infallibility to original sin, despite disquiet in "certain modern quarters."

Speaking on the fifth anniversary of his coronation and at the closing ceremony of the Year of Faith, Pope Paul expressed concern over "a kind of passion for change and novelty" that has been troubling the church.

In a separate message to priests of the world many of whom "feel that they have been thrust aside by modern social developments," the Pontiff reaffirmed the importance of clerical celibacy and of priests' role among youth and workers.

The Pope delivered the 3000-word "Credo of the People of God" to a crowd of 40,000 in St. Peter's Square.

It was the most comprehensive pronouncement on faith of the Pope's reign.

"We have wished our profession of faith to be to a high degree complete and explicit, in order that it may respond in a fitting way to the need of light felt by so many faithful souls."

He reaffirmed faith in the oneness of God and the mystery of the Trinity, Jesus Christ as the Son of God, the virginity of

Mary and her role in the church's moral life and the concept
of original sin as common to all men.

He also listed the importance of baptism, the Roman Catholic
Church as the only true church, the need for a church hierar-
chy, infallibility of the Pope and of bishops as a body under the
Pontiff, the Mass as a real reenactment of Christ's death, the
Eucharist as the true body and blood of Jesus and the existence
of paradise, purgatory and hell.

Associated Press [2]

In government there is a general distinction to be made
between questions having to do with structure and those having to do with action. The first is the sphere of constitution.
The second is the sphere of process. In law there is a differentiation between "constitutional" and "political" matters.
It is instructive that the Supreme Court of the United States
concerns itself with "constitutional" cases, but avoids "political" ones. The particular reasons for this are complex, including the constitutional guarantees of division of powers between
legislative, executive, and judicial branches of government.
However, this may also be an implicit recognition that the dynamics of political life do not lend themselves to neat legal
categorization, an admission that political action is a "law unto
itself," with nuances and delicate balances which do not precisely conform to constitutional niceties, and yet which are
essential to the effective functioning of the body politic. Constitution, in this sense, is in the realm of reason; politics is in
the realm of mystery.

In an analogous way, it is possible to distinguish between
the polity and the politics of the church. Polity has to do with
its structure. Politics has to do with its dynamics. Or, to use
more classical terms, it is in part the difference between form
and spirit, or, in another context, between letter and spirit.
It must be admitted, nevertheless, that though this conceptual distinction can be, and is, made, in actual practice the two
spheres intermesh. As Ernst Cassirer writes: "every concept
has a 'certain area' that belongs to it and whereby it is distin-

guished from other conceptual spheres. No matter how much these areas may overlap, cover each other or interpenetrate— each one maintains its definitely bounded location in concep- tual space. A concept maintains its sphere despite all its syn- thetic supplementation and extension; the new relations into which it may enter do not cause its boundaries to become ef- faced, but lead rather to their more distinct recognition."[3]

Thus, for the sake of analysis, we may concentrate on the polity of the church without forgetting, nonetheless, that it is inseparably connected with its politics. We may address ourselves to the form of the church, without forgetting that its spirit is inextricably involved. Or, to put it another way, we may separate polity and politics without losing sight of the fact that "politics" in its highest and most comprehensive defini- tion encompasses both.

The difficulty of expounding this interrelationship is cor- relative with the difficulty the church has found in making this distinction in its actual existence, historically and today. What *is* the relation, for example, between the essential na- ture of the church and its external form? What is the connec- tion between its life and its embodiment or embodiments? Again we may say that these are distinguishable but not sep- arable. There is no nature without a form and there is no life without an embodiment.

This leads, however, to another question. To what extent does the form of the church correspond to its essential nature? It is conceptual confusion at this point that may be the source of many of the ecclesiological controversies that recur in church history and are evident in current ecumenical debates. For it is one thing to say that a form of the church *is* an expression of its spirit; it is another thing to say that this form *must be* the expression or reflection of its spirit and nature. The one state- ment is what might be called incarnational realism; the other is institutional fundamentalism. The one is an admission of the need for the formal in life. The other is formalism. The one is realistic about the necessity of formal expression. The other is obsessed by this necessity to the extent that it becomes a fixation. In the latter case, there is a formalistic identification of a particular embodiment or structure or concept with the spirit, life, and idea that these represent.

Cassirer calls this type of fusion in thinking "mythic." As he says, "Here we find in operation a law which might actually be called the law of the leveling and extinction of specific differences. Every part of a whole is the whole itself. . . . The Pythagoreans still observed the injunction to smooth the bed soon after arising so that the imprint of the body, left upon the mattress, could not be used to the owner's detriment. Most of what is known as 'magic of analogy' springs from the same fundamental attitude; and the very nature of this magic shows that the concept in question is not one of mere analogy, but of a real identification. . . . it is equally clear that for mythic thinking there is much more in metaphor than a bare 'substitution,' a mere rhetorical figure of speech; that what seems to our subsequent reflection as a sheer transcription is mythically conceived as a genuine and direct identification. . . . This is more obviously valid if we consider that for mythic and magical thought there is no such thing as a *mere* picture, since every image embodies the 'nature' of its object, i.e., its 'soul' or 'daemon.'"[4]

This chapter's two cases may have at least this much in common: They both vividly exhibit this metaphoric, "mythic" thinking. Such Pythagorean conservatism, one in regard to religion and the other in regard to sex, may derive from the same conceptual fallacy—the inability to distinguish between analogy and identification, between figure and idea. And, in a certain symbolic way, this "straitlaced" mentality goes on to an even deeper identification. The personalities involved, partly through the subtle skills of public relations and media magicians, are identified as the real "soul" of that which they symbolically represent. Thus the Pope *is* Church. Or, as Cassirer puts it: "The mental view is not widened, but compressed; it is, so to speak, distilled into a single point. Only by this process of distillation is the particular essence found and extracted which is to be the special accent of 'significance.' All light is concentrated in one focal point of 'meaning,' while everything that lies outside these focal points of verbal or mythic conception remains practically invisible."[5]

It would be fascinating, though outside the scope of this chapter, to pursue this line of thought in analyzing the dogma of infallibility itself. That is, the idea of the doctrinal authority of the church becomes identified with a particular form of expression of that authority, or, focused on one spokesman, concentrated in one individual. Or, from another perspective, a special theological "reading" of the Nicene Creed, as in Pope Paul's "Credo," becomes identified with the Creed itself. As the Archbishop of Canterbury, Dr. Arthur Michael Ramsey, noted at the 1968 Assembly of the World Council of Churches: "Since the Vatican Council began to distinguish between the more fundamental dogmas and the less fundamental ones, I was surprised that particular Roman Catholic dogmas, like the immaculate conception and papal infallibility, were inserted along with the tenets of the Nicene Creed."

This same kind of "mythic compression" in theology is seen in certain types of Protestant confessionalism. Doctrinal orthodoxy is identified with certain confessional formulations. These formulas then become absolutized. The special historical, cultural, and philosophical factors that have shaped them are lost sight of, "practically invisible," and they come to be considered authoritative in themselves. Rather than being viewed as models, or analogies, of the church's teaching authority in regard to doctrine, their form itself is invested with this authoritative character. The same is true, of course, of biblical fundamentalism in which the authority of the Bible is not understood in this metaphorical way, but literally. Its very form becomes its significance.

The same type of mentality is sometimes exhibited in relation to the polity of the church. It is apparently assumed that the church has only one external form—admittedly modified to meeting changing circumstances or adapted to various environments—and this essential form will remain constant throughout history. Behind this lies the assumption that the image is identical with the nature of the church.

It is, however, apparent that though there is a stubborn persistence of the form of the church down through the centuries—in the Catholic, Protestant, and Orthodox traditions—this may well be due to historical, nontheological factors and not something intrinsic to the essential being of the church as such. It may be, for example, that the hierarchical structure of the church, claimed to be divinely inspired and instituted, persists through history not as a result of this supernatural character but because, as sociologists and political economists infer, hierarchy is indigenous to all institutions and the ability of an institution to survive depends in part on the viability of the particular hierarchical structure it adopts. This is not to deny that the foundation of the church is divinely ordained, but to argue that this ordination is not identical with the political form or forms the church has taken in history.

"The author of the first great treatise on government and politics known to history found it necessary to analyze, compare, and contrast over one hundred and fifty polities and their constitutions as a basis for his conclusions."[6] In so doing, Aristotle is suggesting that whatever one may make of the "state" as to its immutable and eternal character, there are a great variety of polities which can give expression to and articulate this in practical government. And so in the church, differences in polity, either through the course of history or between various Christian bodies at a particular time, are not necessarily indicative of concomitant differences in regard to theological assumptions about the divine nature of the church itself. Two ecclesiastical bodies may have different political forms to express the same ecclesiological doctrine. The various "rites" of the Catholic Church (of which the Roman is only one) is an example of this fact. And in Protestantism there are a number of different polities extant which reflect common theological convictions about the essential nature of the church and its purposes. In Lutheranism, to take another example, one finds both episcopal and nonepiscopal polities in the same communion. Even in churches with only one basic polity—for instance, those with episcopal order—there may be a number of different ways in which the episcopate is politically selected or in which the episcopal functions are politically exercised.

All this argues that polity is a variable determined, on one hand, by the dogmatic self-image of an ecclesiastical body and, on the other hand, by external "nontheological" factors which are sociologically and historically conditioned. Thus, though there is an integral connection between the faith and order of a church, this is not to be understood in such a simplistic manner that any particular order is considered to be the invariable institutional, organizational, or governmental "shape" of the faith. The political form of the church, therefore, though it presumably should reflect and express the faith, is not identical with it.

An analysis of four related concepts—*formation, deformation, reformation,* and *transformation*—may clarify the meaning of this principle in church politics.

The history of the development of church order illustrates this interplay of theological and nontheological—or perhaps more accurrately put: dogmatic and transtheological—factors. The formation of the Christian community mirrors its faith; the shape that it takes reflects its theological self-image. The primitive communism evidenced in the book of Acts, "all who believed were together and had all things in common," is not only a testimony to their common belief but also to their awareness that in some mysterious way their fellowship was a first-fruit of the eschatological realm of Israel, a fulfillment of the long-expected restoration of the coming Kingdom of God foreseen by the fathers and the prophets. Even in this egalitarian ethos, however, there are structural elements. The church is also related to the original band of Jesus' disciples; and thus, by lots, a follower by the name of Matthias is chosen to fill out the vacancy left by Judas in the Twelve. The citation of a verse from the Psalms to justify this procedure—"His office let another take"—is an indication of the importance placed on historical continuity not only with the original band of disciples but also with the Old Testament tradition.

At the same time it must be noted that according to the earliest documentary sources available to us the formation of the church cannot simply be explained as the logical institutional and organizational extension of its faith, the pure political form of its doctrinal tenets and its creedal affirmations. The world in which the church takes form is itself a formative factor in the development of the church's polity.

The search for an authoritative pattern of church organization in the New Testament is, of course, a proverbially difficult task. In part this derives from hermeneutical differences about the way the New Testament is to be regarded as "authority" in such matters. In any case, the best we may be able to do at the moment is to accept the conclusion of Eduard Schweizer: "There is no such thing as *the* New Testament Church order. Even in New Testament times circumstances were very varied, and it may be vital for the ecumenical dialogue that we should admit this."[7]

But admitting the inconclusive position modern biblical scholarship leaves us in, it is still possible to draw out certain significant facts from the New Testament evidence which may be illuminating for our subject. For instance, it is a truism that Jesus' life and ministry is carried out in the context of the religious institutions of that day and that the very form of his passion and death is determined by both the polity of the Jewish religious community and the politics involved in its legal relations with the Roman government. As Schweizer says: "The end of the journey is the cross on which Jesus is executed—outwardly the victory of priesthood and pharisaism, but in fact the end of both."[8] This obviously has both theological and political implications.

When one moves out of the Synoptics, however, and the shape of the church begins to emerge in a shadowy and fragmentary way—as through a glass, darkly—both the polity and the politics of the new Christian community are increasingly delineated. But the political "feel" of this community is more evident than its constitutional form, or polity.

We begin to get vivid glimpses of how it actually operated— that is, of its political ethos, to follow the terminology of this book, or, to put it in another way, we catch vivid reflections of its institutional spirit—even when the exact structure of polity is not apparent.

To take one example: the picture of the church which emerges from the accounts of the Jerusalem Council in Acts and in Paul's writings is that of a dynamic institution full of political vitality. Its explosive missionary expansion has posed a crucial institutional dilemma for the Christian community: can a new form of polity be found which can incorporate the new "strange" elements being offered to it by the missionary labors of the apostles among the Gentiles? The *way* in which this problem is met and dealt with exhibits the politics of the primitive church. Though it is a precarious enterprise to assign our current labels, or to assume too close an approximation to our contemporary categories, in these matters, there are some indications of the political temper of this community worth mentioning. For one thing, sharp differences of opinion and conviction are recognized and expressed within the community: we might say, there is freedom of thought. Debate presupposes this and there was obviously considerable debate leading up to the convening of the Council; in fact, there was "fierce dissension and controversy" (Acts 15:2). For another thing, it seems to be assumed that the resolution of such differences requires corporate consultation and discussion by the community: we might say, the conciliar principle is accepted. Yet another point, when the "apostles and elders held a meeting to look into this matter" (which might be held to be an expression of both a hierarchical and a representative principle of government) there was "long debate": we might say, there is freedom of speech. A decision is reached by common consent involving compromise but "unanimously" accepted by all parties: we might say, democratic policy is applied. Finally, the new agreement is codified and this consensus sent to the outlying congregations: we might say, a responsible and informed constituency is thought to be essential to the well-being of the body. Thus we see the institutionalization of the Christian community taking place *through* its political activities.

Is church order divinely ordained or humanly contrived? In the book *Apostolic Ministry* certain church union schemes are criticized because, it is argued, in them the church is not regarded "as a wonderful and sacred mystery, a life carrying its own law of development within it."[9] By this logic, the similarities of ecclesiastical and secular organization are only apparent or accidental. At the other extreme, in the controversial Bampton Lectures of 1880, Edwin Hatch argued that church organization is fundamentally "natural," that "the elements of which that organization was composed were already existing in human society."[10] T. M. Lindsay, though not so extreme, yet sees influences from at least five sources in the development of early church organization: *(i)* Jerusalem religious life; *(ii)* Jewish village government—e.g., the "Seven"; *(iii)* general Oriental customs—e.g., "line of succession, from eldest male surviving relative to eldest male surviving relative"; *(iv)* Roman example—e.g., the confraternities or *"scholae"; (v)* synagogue organization.[11]

In any case, as early as the second century, the church was "almost a replica in miniature of a Roman municipality. It had a body of officers, graded like those of the city, clothed in similar vestments and bearing similar titles."[12] Lindsay points out the same thing: that the early orders of clergy were based on the model of organization of the state temple service; the imperial cult was copied, and then supplanted, by the Christian churches, so that by the fourth century this similarity was such that when "the time of the Church's triumph came, as it did early in the century, very little change of previous state arrangements was needed to install the new religion in place of the old."[13] The church, in short, had not only blended into its environment: it had digested it—not without, it must be admitted, some severe institutional cramps and political pangs. The church had a spiritual price to pay for its "triumph" and it is, of course, a continuing bone of contention as to whether the price paid was not exorbitant.

But, however that may be argued, it cannot be denied that practical exigencies forced the development of church organization. For one thing, from the time when the apostles were the sole directors and administrators, with responsibility for both financial and spiritual guidance, the situation gradually developed when the "work became too vast and too various for them to discharge unaided" and to "relieve them from increasing pressure, the inferior and less important functions passed successively into other hands; and thus each grade of the ministry." For another, as Bishop Lightfoot also suggested, the very catholic organization of the church was a response to a functional need: "With the overthrow of Jerusalem the visible center of the Church was removed. The keystone of the fabric was withdrawn, and the whole edifice threatened with ruin. There was a crying need for some organization which should cement together the diverse elements of Christian society and preserve it from disintegration."[14] E. F. Scott summarizes this functional interpretation with the thesis that the visible organization of the church was determined by two key factors: *(i)* "the material needs of the community"; *(ii)* "the growing success of the mission which compelled the church to organize."[15]

Perhaps the chief lesson to be drawn from this somewhat kaleidoscopic picture is simply that the church was not only forced to organize but that it was forced to develop more and more complicated forms of organization. Organization, in brief, was required for survival, and, one might add, effective ecumenical organization for expansion and growth. There can be little argument that the organization of the early church derived from many sources and influences. The same factors are determinative in the development of modern church organization. Many of the conflicts in respect to church order arise from not recognizing the importance of all these factors, or from stressing only one to the exclusion of the others.

But all this raises a further question, one which is closer to the heart of the problem of modern church organization. It has to do not so much with *what* the early church did, but *why* and *how* it did it. As C. H. Turner, the English church historian, put it: "it is superfluous to ask whether this or that institution is or is not primitive; we should rather ask whether all that was primitive was intended to be permanent."[16] Or to put it another way, the problem is not so much that the church copied so many secular forms and patterns for its organization, but what *principles* of organization lay behind this practice of borrowing and adapting, of conforming and transforming?

There are obviously no easy answers to these questions. Even when the church, at a given period, believes it is structured according to some divinely ordained pattern, history shows the extent to which it has always been an organizational-child-of-its-times. Or to revert to our original distinction between polity and politics, even though the former may be doctrinally oriented, the latter tends to be sociologically determined. Then the two may be confused, so that both the structure of formal polity and the actual political dynamics are thought to be divinely ordained and sanctioned. And this confusion is compounded when particular forms of politics are thought to be divine, and therefore immutable, rather than historically conditioned and sociologically relative expressions of certain principles of church order, certain truths about the nature of Christian community, and, not least, certain facts about the nature of man and society.

A defect of much traditional church history is that though it provides us with fairly clear pictures of how the church looked in a constitutional sense in earlier times, it often does not give us much of an idea of how it actually operated in a political way. Adolf Harnack says the primitive church in the New Testament "with its simplicity and naturalness, proved itself extraordinarily strong." But as that original simplicity of form evolved into an ordered hierarchy and eventually, by the end of the second century, into the organization of a catholic episcopate accepted throughout the church, its continued strength seems in part at least due to the fact that the church was willing to leave the primitive "simplicity" of organization behind it. There was a certain political dynamism within the Christian community which seemed to be able to adapt itself to, and transform, the successive stages of polity and also to provide a living continuity between these changing forms which these forms in themselves apparently lacked.

One sees this partially in the evolution of the juridical organization of the church in the movement from local to provincial to league of provinces to collective church, with the increasing centralization that implied. In the Chalcedon (A.D. 451) Canons 9 and 17, for example, provision is made for an exarch to be the tribunal of appeal in cases involving controversy with a metropolitan. This underlines the growing complexity of church organization in the period from Nicaea in A.D. 325 to Chalcedon in which dioceses grouped into provinces, provinces into exarchates, and exarchates were partially grouped and partially superseded by the partriarchates. The whole story might be summed up in the words of Streeter: "the Church was an organism alive and growing—changing its organization to meet changing needs—the system of government varied from church to church, and in the same church at different times."[17]

But the very political vitality of the church created its own problems. Over the centuries there was an underlying tension between "autocratic" and "democratic" political ideals, and though Cyprian apparently resolved this struggle between the "primitive democratic organization" and the "representative ecumenical council or synod" with his autocratic conception of the episcopacy, the two political theories existed side by side from the third to the tenth century, to revive again during the Reformation. In this perspective, we can understand that Cyprian's "high" doctrine of the episcopacy is not simply the evolutionary apex of the development of an increasingly centralized polity, as for example in the growing authority of the metropolitans at the expense of both local congregations and synodical councils, but the articulation of the theological confusion between the church as a God-given institution and the particular, historical institutional forms being decrees of God, and beyond that the assumption that the theological rationalization of polity can and will resolve basic political differences. In short, the changes which necessity demanded, and in which external factors played a decisive role, became theologically and doctrinally sanctioned; and not only sanctioned, but petrified against further change.

It is precisely here—as it became in the time of the Reformation—that the question of *deformation* emerges as critical. For what criteria are to be used to decide what is true formation and what is actual deformation? As E. F. Scott remarks: "While changing itself into a worldly institution it yet magnified its title to be above the world. It required all these things which belonged to its outward organization—ceremonies, offices, buildings, robes and insignia—should be accounted holy. They had been borrowed from the world, to adapt the church to earthly conditions, and now they were revered for their own sake, as part of the higher order." On the other hand, as he admits, though the church may have surrendered much in the process and became "in many ways a loser . . . [yet] if it had failed to organize itself the Church could not have survived.' [18]

Bishop Lightfoot in his essay on "The Christian Ministry" makes much the same point. From the theological side one may view the church as the embodiment of the Kingdom of Christ which "is in the fullest sense free, comprehensive, universal" and, yet, it is "evident that no society of men could hold together without officers, without rules, without institutions of any kind; and the Church of Christ is not exempt from this universal law. In this respect the ethics of Christianity present an analogy to the politics. Here also the ideal conception and the actual realization are incommensurate and in a manner contradictory."[19]

Ironically, therefore, the very polities and politics required by the church for its survival, the very formations demanded in order to maintain itself as a viable institution are also potentially the source and the cause of its deformation. From this viewpoint "it is not surprising," as E. F. Scott notes, "that later reformers in almost every age have fixed on the organization of the Church as the prime cause of all its errors."[20]

This may be explained in part by the fact that organization incarnates and expresses the deepest and most fundamental convictions about the ultimate nature of the church. This may be seen in Luther's revolt, which is often interpreted exclusively as a theological reaction against the doctrinal errors of the Roman Church of his day but which, as a re-reading of such basic Reformation writings as "Address to the Christian Nobility" reveals, is also focused on the institutional forms of the church; they are seen as visible and evident signs of the theological abuses and heresies which he sought to correct. In this sense, he was quite literally the "re-*former*"—in spirit and intention, if not always in practice.

But Luther also represents the revival of a philosophy of church politics which ran counter to that of the Roman Catholic ecclesiastical establishment. Just as the Montanist movement was "on its practical side . . . equally a rebound from the aggressive tyranny of hierarchical assumption"[21] and was thus a political protest, so Luther and the Reformers who followed embodied and articulated a revolution in political thinking current in that day in the secular sphere, *within* the church. Luther did not object to the idea of a Roman Catholic Church, but to how it operated politically. He did not reject bishops, but he denounced their political methods. He could tolerate the polity of the Roman Church, but only if it expressed the political dynamics of the theological revolution he was preaching. Luther, in short, represented the continuity of dynamic church politics (in historic succession to Marsiglio of Padua) over against the formal and petrified institutionalism of the late medieval Roman establishment. And the only resolution of this classical tension could be reformation—or schism.

This may be illustrated by Luther's approach to canon law. Although his scathing attacks on it are well known, the bases of his criticisms are less familiar. He does not attack law or legal institutions in themselves, but their abuse and corruption. Law has its proper function and purpose in the social and political and ecclesiastical sphere. The trouble with the Roman Church of his time, as he pointed out to the German nobility, was that "the canon law contains so many heretical and unchristian, nay unnatural laws"; his criterion for judging ecclesiastical laws was that they "hold good only so long as they are not injurious to Christianity and the laws of God." In the same way, he is not, as is sometimes assumed, completely anarchical in his view of church institutions. The "third wall" erected by the Roman Church against reform was, according to Luther, the doctrine "that no one may call a council but the Pope." To this his answer is not that councils are unimportant or unnecessary—on the contrary, he placed great importance on them—but such a truly ecumenical council means "I must collect the Church together" and, should the position of the Pope himself be at stake, "in these cases whoever can best do so, as a faithful member of the whole body, must do what he can to procure a true free council."[22]

In other words, he was arguing for a more democratic and responsible church politics (to use modern terminology) over against an oligarchical and autocratic and even tyrannical political system. And if in this he is the forerunner of a whole new movement in Christian history, he is at the same time the embodiment of a very ancient tradition of Catholic church politics—one which is only today once again being expressed and championed in the Roman Catholic Church, at the same time, ironically, when it seems to be increasingly obscured and forgotten in Protestantism itself.

This underlines the fact that a radical spirit in regard to church politics *may* be combined with a conservative approach to church polity, a combination which is seen in Wesley as well as Luther. Of course, both Luther and Wesley represent examples of the tragedy when the church does not have the institutional flexibility to comprehend politically charismatic movements. If the institutional "squeeze" on such supercharged political forces becomes too severe through suppression or persecution, an explosion is inevitable and the unity of polity is destroyed. Happier examples can be cited of the ability of the church to exhibit political sensitivity and institutional flexibility—for instance, in the case of monasticism or the Jesuits —but when, as with the Lutheran or Wesleyan movements, the church feels threatened by a fear that the political forces of independence and devolution directed against the established polity are of such magnitude and intensity as to overturn its order and the *status quo,* a radical break between the old polity and the new politics is almost inevitable.

From the opposite side, the reformers are also often guilty of this same type of oversimplification of the relation between faith and order. It is one thing to detect that the organization of the church is a prime cause of many of its deformations. It is another to assert that it is "the prime cause of *all* its errors." To put the matter in a more modern frame of reference, it is a commonplace that institutionalization is a bad thing. But is institutionalization bad *per se?* Or is it even the prime cause of the deformation of the church? From this point of view, it would be logical to argue that the church should not be an institution at all, that it need have no order, that it required no organization, that it does not have to have a structure. That, of course, is the classical docetic heresy in ecclesiological form.

Strangely enough, some of the sociological studies of church organization have seemed to encourage this attitude and, indeed, have in certain cases appeared to exhibit the bias. On one side, therefore, the sociologist demonstrates that the church is a human institution and, on the other, blames the church for that fact. So, a kind of sociological overkill has taken place. In many circles, the revelation that the church reverberates with the "noise of solemn assemblies" or is apparently imprisoned in a "suburban captivity" or has become a "stained-glass jungle" is not taken to mean that deformation is possible in the church and that there are a variety of ways in which this can happen, but that the church is betrayed by being found in any visible, identifiable form at all.

This anti-institutional spirit is a part of the critical, iconoclastic—one might almost say, Gnostic—attitude. It is found in secular forms in regard to government or business. And it is found in the church. Such critiques of the polity of the church are, admittedly, both appropriate and healthy when they draw attention to the discrepancies between the church's affirmations and its actions, between its faith and its life. As Martin Marty summarized the "final indictment" of Walter Kaufmann's book *The Faith of a Heretic:* "The churches are preaching against bad faith, dishonesty, poor ethics, immorality—and at the same time, through their self-seeking institutionalism, they are serving to promote bad faith, dishonesty, poor ethics, immorality."[23] But to imply that such a betrayal is intrinsic to institutionalization as such is to invalidate the critique. Furthermore, such a conclusion is ultimately destructive to any kind of constructive or reformative response. Eventually it leads to complete political passivity and social fatalism.

The "bigness" and "bureaucratic" nature of modern large-scale church polity has drawn a great deal of critical fire. But this is only one part of *The Dilemma of Organizational Society,* as the book by that title edited by H. M. Ruitenbeck vividly illustrates.[24] A dilemma is, in any case, not necessarily the equivalent of damnation. Harland Cleveland in arguing a "Case for Bureaucracy: Exposing Six 'Myths,'" admits that to "most of us 'bureaucracy' is an I-don't-like-it word." Two of the "myths" he discounts are: "Huge bureaucracies are impossible to administer," and "Bureaucracies stifle initiative and smother the individual with the sheer weight of their bigness." "Not impossible," he retorts to the first canard, "—just difficult. Bigness does put a premium on leadership, and the bigger the organization, the more its whole performance depends on who's in charge." To the second, he replies: "Nonsense. A drone is a drone, in large enterprises or small. Drones can make large organizations 'bureaucratic,' but bureaucracy does not make men drones. Our environment is full of big organizations. Just as the cave man had to learn to live in his environment so did people at each succeeding level of social organization. Nowadays, the people who are stifled, frustrated and unhappy about bureaucracies are those who have never bothered to learn enough about their environment to swim freely around in it." His conclusion: "Not everybody is built for the bureaucratic jungle—nor did every cave man survive in the jungles of long ago. But big bureaucracy is here to stay. Every time science turns up something new and big for us to do, we wrap another large organization around the new discovery, to contain and exploit it. When Telstar relayed its first signal, we knew we could build a global system of communications satellites; we also knew we would have to build a global bureaucracy to manage the system. So it goes. Big bureaucracy—public and private—is merely part of the social fallout of scientific discovery and technological advance. We are still committed to the idea that government should be no bigger than it has to be. But we are also committed to the Lincolnian precept that government should do for the people what the people cannot do, or cannot do as well, for themselves. And that will continue to mean bureaucratic structures large enough and baffling enough to draw fire from those magazine writers and others who have yet to catch up with Lincoln."[25]

Thus, to come to terms with the problem of church polity in a perceptive and creative way, both formalistic and docetic modes of thought have to be abandoned. Both, though in opposite directions, prejudge the issue. The formalist assumes that polity remains constant, or ought to, and therefore the question of the *deformation* of polity never arises. The Doce-tist assumes that polity is essentially wrong and therefore the *question* of deformation is irrelevant.

The position espoused here is political realism. That is, the polity of the church has to be approached in dynamic cate-gories in order to do justice to the constantly changing circum-stances and conditions of life. It has to be approached in in-carnational categories in order to do justice to the fact that the church exists in this world and not outside it.

Politics is functionally oriented. That is, it is concerned with relating means to ends. It may be, then, that a political perspective provides a useful criterion for distinguishing au-thentic formation from deformation. A form—whatever form—authenticates itself by its political viability. Concomitantly, deformation is that which is dysfunctional.

This principle should not be interpreted in too narrow, or cynical, a manner. Politics, in its highest form, is not only concerned with how to get things done, or in what ways cer-tain goals can be reached. It is also concerned about what those goals are and the appropriateness of the means of getting things done to those ends. Thus, the criterion for judging between true form and deformation would incorporate within itself a recognition of the ideological self-image of the political body concerned—its faith; an awareness of the historical anteced-ents of which it is custodian—its tradition; an appreciation of its ultimate goals—its hope; a sense of its essential spirit—its vitality; an understanding of its unique character—its char-ter. With these well in mind, and with a realistic assessment of the environment and the resources available, the politician must then shape a polity which does justice to both these ideo-logical and material factors. Thus, a viable polity is one that is functionally effective both in regard to symbolizing the es-sential nature of the body and in facilitating that body in main-taining its ongoing life and in achieving its ultimate purposes.

It is this "reshaping" task which is involved in *reforma-tion* and *transformation*. The latter term suggests, as has been previously mentioned, that true politics is not only a science but also an art. For to project and realize a viable and functional polity is much more than a technical or mechanical enterprise. In fact, part of the art is the ability to discern when reformation may be adequate to correct the deformation, and when transformation is required. For reformation suggests a more conservative, a less radical, type of correction than does transformation. The latter implies a comprehensive change in which very little, if any, of the previous form is preserved and in which, externally, the formal continuity between the old embodiment and the new may be practically nonexistent. It would be in nature analogous to the continuity of the seed and the plant, for example. Reformation might be considered analogous to the modifications in plant structure through evolutionary development—for instance, the evolving of smaller leaf surfaces for survival in arid environments.

A comparison with a similar distinction in architecture may make the difference somewhat more sharply marked. Frank Lloyd Wright, the architectural pioneer, held as two of his basic tenets that "form follows function" and that architecture should be "organic." As to the first, he argued that form, as in nature, should be functional. It should not determine the function, or restrict or limit it, but should be expressive of it. The shape of a house, for instance, should be decided by its function or functions; the shape of a factory by its proposed use; the form of a church by its purpose, and so on. Thus, deformation is the product of a reversal of the order; function follows form. The extent of deformation is proportional to the degree that function follows form; the measure of true form is the purity with which it embodies and fulfills the function. Thus, Wright's definition of style is: "power directly applied to purpose."

The second article of his creed is closely allied: "the idea of life itself—bodily and spiritually—intrinsic *organism*. Form and function as one." By this he means that, in the "new architectural freedom" he advocates, "buildings may proceed *from within outward.* . . . To sum up, organic architecture sees the third dimension never as weight or mere thickness but always as depth. Depth an element of space; the third (or thickness) dimension transformed to a *space* dimension . . . a true liberation of life and light within walls; a new structural integrity; outside coming in; and the space within, to be lived in, going out. Space outside becomes a natural part of space *within* the building." It is interesting that Wright believed that this principle was first realized in a church building: "The first conscious expression of which I know in modern architecture of this *new reality*—the 'space within to be lived in'—was Unity Temple in Oak Park."[26]

It has already been seen in the history of the growth of church polity that the order and organization of the Christian community has been realized through a combination of three elements: 1. Imitation; 2. Improvisation; 3. Innovation. The first two have been most characteristic of the way in which Western Christendom has developed its ecclesiastical institutions and structures. Western Christian polities have generally shown an external, formal continuity through history. At the time of the Reformation this formal continuity was fractured. Nevertheless, even in Protestantism this continuity has been maintained. This is, of course, particularly evident in such communions as the Anglican and the Lutheran, where the episcopal and liturgical models of Western Catholicism have been followed both through imitation and improvisation. In left-wing Protestantism there has been more radical innovation in polity, though even here (as Ernest Troeltsch's *Social Teachings of the Christian Church* shows) the models of pre-Reformation "sect-type" groups within and on the fringe of established Catholicism, such as monasticism and the orders, may provide the visible line of formal continuity.

In any case, reformation has been the typical mode of reshaping and restructuring the polity of the church to meet changing conditions and to adapt to new environments. And, on the whole, the reforming movements in Western Christianity have been largely conservative in intent, if not in achievement. Furthermore, even in radical Protestantism, the posture has been retrospective. In this case, the rationale has been to reform by going back to "primitive" models in the New Testament and the early church. The continuity principle has not been abandoned, but there is a kind of historical leap-frog process whereby the immediate preceding models are rejected in favor of those of more ancient vintage.

The point to be noted here is that reformation as a mode of change generally operates with the underlying assumption that continuity is sustained on the formal, external level. There may be substantial disagreement between reformers and reforming groups about what that formal line of continuity is or how it is to be currently expressed, but the principle that there is a formal connection between the past, or "original," formation and the present reformation remains unchallenged.

Phenomenologically this may well be so. History chronicles this formal continuity between the old forms and the "new" in the Western tradition. On the other hand, as the quotation from Karl Rahner already cited indicates, this type of continuity may be explained in large measure by historical and sociological continuity of the environment of the Western church, both Catholic and Protestant. In other words, the formal continuity of polity may be largely *accidental,* in a literal sense, deriving from the similarity of the historical, sociological environment which is a contributing, often decisive, factor in shaping the polity of the church.

But what if the environment is radically altered? What if the continuity between the old environment and the new is so profoundly broken that there is very little external connection between the two? In the context of this kind of *revolutionary* change—as distinct from *evolutionary*—reformation may be an inadequate, indeed irrelevant, response to the problem of realizing new forms in the new order. Or at the least one might suspect that the reforming intent of maintaining *formal* continuity with the past may at best be a kind of rearguard action which may delay the impact of the new order's emergence but cannot in the last analysis withstand its revolutionary force.

In short, the appropriateness of reformation as a means of maintaining the viability of the polities of the church is dependent on the extent of the continuity of the environment which helped to shape the original forms. This kind of assessment of the situation is part of the science and art of politics. And it is the political problem not only to make this kind of analysis but to determine the kind of reformation required as well as to devise the means for achieving it. Thus the Consultation on Church Union confronts the question of the appropriate structure for the new church: "The reiterated insistence that the united church must be flexible and able to evolve new structures to meet new demands seems to reflect a dissatisfaction among members of all the churches in the Consultation with the difficulties of their present organizations in finding ways to deal with changes taking place in our cities, with mobile populations, with the needs of the poor and of minority groups, with the kinds of questions young people ask today."[27] Will reformation be enough?

Or Hans Küng, following Karl Rahner, as a spokesman for the group of modern Catholic "reformers" raises fundamental questions about the papacy as the epitome of Roman polity: "The chief difficulty in the way of reunion lies in the two different concepts of the Church, and especially of the concrete organizational structure of the Church. We could, no doubt, reach agreement on many fundamental, dogmatic statements about the nature of the Church. . . . We might reach agreement not only in words but on their meaning, until we came to the question (which nevertheless determines the sense of all these expressions) of the Church's concrete organizational structure. And this is in no sense a purely external question; here are rooted all our still unresolved problems about the binding nature of ecclesiastical tradition. . . . Ultimately, all questions about the concrete organizational structure of the Church are crystallized in the question of *ecclesiastical office."* Küng argues that in the case of Luther his "central demand" was reformation: "Luther did not want to found a new Church but to reform the old. . . . Hence it came about that Luther, who affirmed the reality of the ecclesiastical office, came into tragic conflict with ecclesiastical office. . . . The *practical* opposition to ecclesiastical office, born of the pressures and compulsions of that historical situation, developed into an opposition *in principle,* directed especially against the Petrine office. The way was to some extent prepared for this opposition in principle by the unclear ecclesiology of Luther and of the age. . . . But without the appalling conditions of ecclesiastical office, and especially that of Peter, at the end of the Middle Ages, which called the opposition into being at the practical level, its erection into a principle would never have been achieved. Today, we are trying, on both sides, to make good the omissions of that time."[28]

As Küng points out, there are a number of ways in which this later reformation is being brought about. For instance, ecclesiastical office, he says "is now being seen primarily not so much as authority but rather as service" and therefore "The man who holds office cannot then regard himself as 'in command' of his office; rather he is bound to exercise it as service . . . not a sense of dominion but a sense of service." Also, there is a new ecclesiological perspective developing which aims "not at simply deducing the Church from the Papacy but at understanding the Papacy from the point of view of the Church."[29] Again it may be asked: Will reformation be enough?

This theological revitalization and reconceptualization, which is an essential precondition of reformation, is a difficult undertaking. Küng notes that in the Protestant Reformation "the *concrete situation* of the Papacy at that time made it impossible to see the *nature* of the Papacy clearly" and, likewise, "it is equally true that all our exegetical and historical researches and discussions on the question *today,* all our theological reflections *today* on the necessity and significance of the Petrine office in the post-apostolic Church, are essentially modified (and, as far as Protestants are concerned, hampered) by the concrete situation of the Papacy *today*."[30]

The Consulation on Church Union acknowledges the same difficulty in following out its guideline that "all structures should be examined and re-examined to determine whether they obstruct or serve well the Church's mission in the contemporary world." As the report says: "This examination will be arduous and will surely result in pain for all the churches which may unite: everyone tends to feel that the 'structures' he is deeply involved in are in truth essential to the work of the Church in the world—and that the way his own pension plan, or congregational government, or adult education program is organized is the best way. No one wants very much to change."[31]

This is a common psychological phenomenon which is normal and understandable. The structural character of man's thinking processes inhibit revisualization and reconceptualization. Nils Bohr, the Nobel prize-winning scientist, said that the new theories in physics do not generally take hold and become accepted by intellectual conversion but only as those who believe the old theories die. This fact may explain why reformation to most individuals and institutions may be a more congenial mode of change—if the necessity of change is granted at all—than transformation. For the latter obviously requires a greater degree of mental reorientation and seems to demand a more radical conceptual revision than the former. It may also explain the bias in the church, and other institutions as well, toward reformation—whether it is appropriate or not—as the means of change.

This mental rigidity effectively forecloses the other options in regard to change. In particular, the dynamic potentialities of the idea of transformation are excluded. The spirit of reformation, then, which is an advance beyond the static posture and attitude of pure formalism, itself may become an inhibiting factor in bringing about change if it also becomes absolutized as a formative principle. In fact, it may only be the old formalism in a more dynamic mode—institutional fundamentalism in disguise, as it were.

A new psychological discipline, Synectics—taken from the Greek, meaning the "joining together of different and apparently irrelevant elements"—is addressing itself to the development of creative capacity, particularly in the analysis of the underlying psychological mechanisms that are basic to creativity. Three of the basic hypotheses of synectic theory are: "*(i)* creative efficiency in people can be markedly increased if they understand the psychological process by which they operate; *(ii)* in creative process the emotional component is more important than the intellectual, the irrational more important than the rational; *(iii)* it is these emotional, irrational elements which can and must be understood in order to increase the probability of success in a problem-solving situation."[32]

Mainly directed toward the technological and organizational facets of business and industry (though clearly not intrinsically limited to that sphere), Synectics seeks to stimulate creativity and attack particular problems by "controlled irrationality." It thereby seeks to produce novel solutions to such problems by bypassing or transcending the logical, rational, systematic "hang-ups" which restrict and delimit human mental innovation. For example, both experience and expertise, valuable as they are in certain areas of life, tend to restrict the range of creative vision and to block off real possibilities which are open, but which because they as yet have not been experienced or foreseen are therefore subconsciously excluded from the calculations. The assumption that reformation is the only way to respond to change, and its corollary assumption that continuity must be formal in character, is just such a restricted prejudgment imposed by expertise and experience, by logic and rationality, on the creative potentialities open to the church in actualizing itself politically.

To avoid these mental rigidities, and the blocks they set up against innovation, Synectics introduces as fully as possible "play" with language and logical pattern. This in part involves, for instance, "making the strange familiar" (e.g., the use of metaphor and parable) as well as "making the familiar strange." W. J. J. Gordon, an authority in synectics research and president of a business consultant firm, the Invention Research Group, explains the latter process: "Making the familiar strange and sustaining that strangeness requires a constant vigilance to reawaken the evocative quality of comparison relationships. It involves achieving new ways to ask old questions: Everybody knows what the word 'open' means. Only by devising a new way to ask the question: 'What does *open* mean?' can we re-project the metaphoric and speculative potential inherent in the universal (open) and in the particulars (examples of *open* and openness) which interplay with that universal."[33]

If the problem is, for example, to create a new roof, "making the strange familiar" will involve an analysis revealing the basic functions as well as the drawbacks of traditional roofs. In "making the familiar strange" the roof is looked at as if it had never been seen before, that is, "foreign" to the familiar observer. By analogical play different kinds of roofs are considered. This example of the synectics process, described by Gordon, in fact led to one group viewing the roof as though it were a flounder's back. And this resulted in a new viewpoint which resulted in a technological breakthrough: "Each time that analogies derived from the use of mechanisms are compared with the problem as understood a new viewpoint is potential, though not necessarily actual. When the comparison is effective in leading to a technical insight into the problem as understood, then the viewpoint is actual. In the roof example, the viewpoint resulting from seeing the roof as a flounder's back did in fact lead to a technical insight about how a roof could be made to change from white to black at the proper intervals."[34]

It would appear that a synectic approach to the problems of church structure and organization, the basic issues of pol-

ity and politics, might well open the way for not only reformation but also, more importantly, for the full potentialities
of transformation. To refer once again to the architectural
analogy, Frank Lloyd Wright points out the continuity of architectural tradition should be realized not formally but functionally. Imitation and transplantation of forms and styles seem
to represent a respect for tradition. So it does, but in a formal, not a functional, way. Functional continuity of tradition
means something quite different: "I suggest that a revival, not
of the Gothic style but of the Gothic spirit, is needed in the
Art and Architecture of the modern life of the world. We all
now need interpretation of the best traditions in the world
but made to match the great Tradition and our own individual methods. We must repulse every stupid attempt to imitate
and fasten ancient forms, however scientific—upon a life that
must outgrow them however great they seem. Reviving the
Gothic-spirit would necessarily not mean using the forms of
Gothic architecture as handed down to us from 'les Moyen
Ages.' It necessarily would mean something quite different.
Conditions and ideals fixing the forms of the twelfth—say—are
not those conditions and ideals that can truthfully (or profit-
ably) fix forms of the amazing mechanization of the Twentieth
Century. The Spirit that fixed those forms will be the Spirit
that will fix the new forms. Classicists and schools will, of
course, proceed to deny the new forms and finding no 'Gothic'
in them scorn and repulse them. It will not much matter. The
new forms—if actual—will be living, doing their work quietly
and effectively until all these borrowed garments now being cut
over to fit by the Academies are cast off."[35]

It is in this sense that Wright, while decrying imitative and
parasitic designs ("bastard-Gothic," "fictitious semblances"),
identifies himself as a "Gothic" architect: "I have called this
modern feeling for the Organic character of form and treatment 'the Gothic spirit' because it was more nearly realized
in forms of that period, perhaps, than in any other period. At
least the infinitely varied forms of Gothic architecture are

often more literally organic. The Spirit in which they were conceived and wrought was usually one of integrity of means to ends. In this Spirit, America—other nations no less—will find forms best suited to her opportunities, aims and her Life."[36]

This understanding of form as vital and organic, and of tradition as functionally defined, liberates the polity of the church from static and formalistic imprisonment. It makes way not only for conservative reformation but for radical transformation of ecclesiastical structures. It lends itself to dynamic politics. It also means that neither the present nor the future are enslaved by the past. Every period and every age, and the forms that it actualizes, has its own integrity. Furthermore, every formation, every polity, has a partial and incomplete character expressive of the fact that we can only "see in a mirror dimly" and we can only "know in part."

When the modern church faces the modern world, therefore, it must be open to the possibility of transformation. A global church cannot operate in an organic and vital way if its polity is basically parochial. Nor can the church minister to the "vertical villages" or the other configurations of contemporary urban culture if its congregational polity is formed, or reformed, on the basis of a structural principle inherited from rural or small-town society. True, the church must manifest the classical "marks" of unity, holiness, catholicity, and apostolicity if it is to assert its identity as church. But these classical marks must be understood in a dynamic way, so that the continuity of tradition is guaranteed by a functional expression of them and not by a static preservation of the forms with which these marks were once identified. The church, in short, must *be* the church, in life and in action, and not just *look* like a church.

Ultimately it is not man's conception of what the polity of the church has been or ought to be that gives the church its form, but the free movement of the Spirit who "blows where he wills." Respect for what God has done in history must be balanced by a lively expectation of what He will do, along with a humble recognition that if the forms of the past and the present do not fulfill his purposes, do not function effectively, He can—if need be—transform the stones of the street into a living temple. Or, as Paul admonishes those who were inclined to rest secure in new patterns of the divine polity—who were absolutizing a new reformation—"do not become proud, but stand in awe. For if God did not spare the natural branches, neither will he spare you. . . . God has the power to graft them in again. For if you have been cut from what is by nature a wild olive tree, and grafted, contrary to nature, into a cultivated olive tree, how much more will these natural branches be grafted back into their own olive tree. . . . For from Him and through Him and to Him are all things." (Rom. 11:20-21, 23-24, 36, RSV).

The polity of the church of the future, as long as there is a future, remains problematical. It is always open. It is constantly in a state of transformation. It is with respect for the past, reverence for the present, and awe for the future that the church must face its problems of polity. As Alfred North Whitehead wrote: "Symbolic transference can achieve miracles of sensitiveness to a distant environment, and to a problematic future." But he warns: "those societies which cannot combine reverence to their symbols with freedom of revision, must ultimately decay either from anarchy, or from a slow atrophy of a life stifled by useless shadows."[37]

The polity of the church should be an expression of freedom—of its own and of the Christian man. The ultimate symbol of the divine polity is the Kingdom of God. The "distant environment" is the *civitas dei.* It is this spiritual community that the polity of the church foreshadows. Thus its polity must always be minimal—that is, its form and structure and organization must be austere, limited to the barest essentials. This is, of course, a basic functional principle. But it also has a symbolic significance. For it means that the church only prefigures the ultimate divine polity: its forms do not in themselves have that eternal character.

Modern architects dream of the "ultimately invisible" architecture: Lönberg-Holm, one of the Bauhaus school, believes that "the greatest architect in history would be the one who finally developed the capacity to give humanity completely effective environment control without any visible structure and machinery."[38] The church, considered as the sacramental sign of the Spirit, living and active, constantly transforming the spiritual community, may achieve freedom in its polity if it understands that it is the creation of just such an architectural imagination and that in fact it does represent "ultimately invisible architecture."

3-*Power*

It Ain't the Heat, It's the Humility

Vatican Attacks 'Foolhardy' Critics

Any refusal by Roman Catholics to accept the Pope's ban on artificial birth control is "foolhardy and scandalous," a Vatican theologian said in Rome yesterday, Reuter reports.

Mgr. Ferdinando Lambruschini, who presented the encyclical on birth control to the press on July 29, said in an article in a Vatican weekly newspaper that the encyclical's teaching was binding on the consciences of all Roman Catholics, both priests and laymen.

The article, entitled The Duty to Agree, added that a Roman Catholic who could not see the reasons for the Pope's decision had no right to challenge it, but must accept it humbly.

"He who refuses the decision of the authentic magistery, and worse still, encourages others to refuse it, is obviously in error. One owes the complete submission of the intelligence and the will to such an authentic pronouncement."

Mgr. Lambruschini attacked dissenting theologians, who, he said, were going against Catholic common sense as well as against the Pope's supreme authority. He wrote: "I wonder in what way these theologians think they are rendering a service to the church—while they are undermining the very basis of its institutions which Jesus Christ desired and laid down."

The Rev. Paul Weir, the Surrey Roman Catholic priest whose

public disagreement with the encyclical led to his suspension from duty, said yesterday that he was unlikely to change his views.

He added: "I am praying for guidance. But my mind is made up on whether contraception is an intrinsic evil."

The officially approved methods of limiting a family "involve very long periods of abstinence from making love which places an unbearable strain on the marriage."

Father Weir, aged 31, has been assistant priest at St. Cecilia's, North Cheam, for the past two years. Parishioners have issued a statement "deploring" his suspension, and 348 have signed a petition in his support.

'Disobedience' led to suspension

The Vicar General of the Southwark archdiocese, Mgr. Gibney, said last night that Father Weir was suspended because of disobedience to his bishop, not for his views on the encyclical.

Mgr. Gibney said: "I asked Father Weir to refrain from talking publicly about the Pope's teaching on birth control and to refrain from giving advice privately. He was unable to give me this assurance, so he had to go." He had made a "last appeal" to Father Weir on Monday.

Acting in the absence of the Archbishop of Southwark, Dr. Cowderoy, Mgr. Gibney had previously suspended Father Weir from preaching and hearing confessions.

"I asked him to take a month off to stop him talking and get him out of the reach of television and newspapers", Mgr. Gibney said. "He was determined to get all the publicity he could for his stand, and it is a pity. He is a nice young man, capable. But you can't do much with these young men."

Asked if Dr. Cowderoy's views on the encyclical did not conflict with those of Cardinal Heenan, head of the Roman Catholic Church in Britain, Mgr. Gibney said the cardinal's pastoral letter had not been very clear.

The letter was meant to tell Roman Catholics that they must follow the encyclical but even if they found this difficult they must still go to the sacraments. So long as they realized that it was wrong to use proscribed contraceptive methods, they could go to confession and get absolution.

Father Weir is still free to practise his religion and can go back to his duties as a priest whenever he gives the required assurances. Mgr. Gibney said several other young priests held the same views as Father Weir.

Father Weir, who will be leaving the presbytery at North Cheam during the next two or three days, has been invited by several parishioners to stay at their homes.

He has been invited by the Rev. David Woodard, parish priest at the church of Our Lady of Peace, Burnham, Buckinghamshire, and his colleagues, the Rev. Nicholas Lash and the Rev. Patrick McDermott, to stay there.

The Bishop of Arundel and Brighton, Mgr. Cashman, is calling two meetings of his priests on September 9 and 10 to discuss the encyclical. His secretary said last night that there was no "element of crisis" about the meetings, but added: "The bishop is aware of the unease which exists among some of his priests."

———

The faculties of hearing confession and preaching have been withdrawn from Rev. Dr. James Good, Professor of Theology at University College, Cork, because of his opposition to the encyclical on birth control.[1]

MERGER AND RACE

Discord Among Methodists

By Lester Kinsolving, Religion Editor

DALLAS.

A Harlem minister stirred the first ripple of discord in the newly merged United Methodist Church here yesterday with a plea for swift and full integration.

It came hard on the heels of a revelation that Bishop Charles Golden of Nashville, a black man who may be the next bishop of the Northern California-Nevada Methodist Conference, was warned against seeking space in the Methodist Publishing House.

The Central Jurisdiction—a special ecclesiastical structure for Methodist blacks—was ordered abolished at the first session of the new church, a giant of Protestantism with some 12 million members.

However, it was decreed that black members be absorbed into the newly [formed] regional conferences—and the conferences of the two merging churches, The Methodist and the Evangelical United Brethren, were given up to 12 years to unite.

The Rev. Roy Nichols of New York, the Harlem black minister, urged faster action—the immediate setting up of an integrated commission to bring the church into the forefront of the struggle for "racial and social justice."

"The white man in the Western world is in trouble," he said.

Rev. Paul A. Duffy of Dothan, Ala., called the proposal "class legislation" and "not a wholesome direction for us at this time."

It was the Central Jurisdiction that gave Nashville two bishops —Golden, the black bishop, and Roy Short, the white bishop.

Bishop Golden confirmed that when he sought space in the $30 million publishing plant, where Bishop Short had an office, he was told by the president, Lovick Pierce, that "there would be little fellowship there."

"I told him I wasn't seeking fellowship, I was seeking space," Bishop Golden said.

Bishop Short thereafter moved out of the building, where black and white workers are assigned separate locker rooms.

"If they don't have space for both bishops, they don't have space for either," Bishop Short said.

Pierce, head of the Methodist Publishing House since 1952, angrily refused to comment on the charges, first raised by the Rev. James R. McGraw of New York.

Bishop Golden contended that "The hold the publishing house has on the Methodist Church is based largely on the fact that it contributes to retired ministers, widows and children. To speak against that is like speaking against motherhood."[2]

A 'Shocker' for Methodist Delegates

By Lester Kinsolving

DALLAS.

Lovick Pierce, president of the Methodist Church's publishing house in Nashville, Tenn., told the General Conference of the United Methodist Church here yesterday that he receives a salary of $55,000.

Pierce's salary disclosure, after the conference's decision to launch an official investigation of the $40 million church publishing house, caused something of a sensation among the delegates, since it amounts to more than three times the $17,500 salary paid to Methodist bishops.

When asked by one delegate about the salaries paid to his fellow executives in the publishing house, Pierce replied: "I don't know for sure. I'd have to guess."

Pierce went on to explain why 71 per cent of the firm's profits were kept for a reserve fund instead of being given to the church clergy pension fund as directed by church law.

The conference accepted the quadrennial report of the Methodist Publishing House, which will be investigated regarding charges of racial discrimination and unfair labor practices. The conference directed the publishing house to include Negro Methodists as staff members.

The conference also upheld the action of its Board of Missions, which withdrew a $10 million investment portfolio from New York's First National City Bank, as a protest against the bank's involvement in a credit arrangement with the government of South Africa.

The board's action was protested by lay delegates John C. Satterfield of Mississippi, a former president of the American Bar Association, and Charles Parlin of New Jersey, a president of the World Council of Churches and a former director of the New York bank.

The decision was defended by the Rev. Eugene Smith of the World Council of Churches, who said that Methodist boards had "a long and stubborn history of scrutinizing their investments."[3]

'MAIN ISSUE'

Grace Cathedral Dean Speaks Out

Episcopal Dean C. Julian Bartlett yesterday said his silence on a resolution concerning finances at the Grace Cathedral should in no way be interpreted as reflecting on the honor and integrity of Bishop C. Kilmer Myers.

Dean Bartlett, speaking to a group of parishioners in an informal "talk-back" session, also confirmed that Bishop Myers had asked him to resign and that he had refused.

Dean Bartlett said "I did not infer an iota on the bishop's honor or integrity by that resolution."

Request

He said he felt at the time it was passed that what was being requested amounted to "a standard business procedure."

Dean Bartlett said he remained silent because he felt the clergy was supposed to remain silent at informal meetings such as the one which passed the resolution.

He said he would have been "on his feet" had he at any time felt the resolution reflected adversely on the bishop's honor or integrity.

Issue

Dean Bartlett said that published reports of his dispute with Bishop Myers "did not treat of the main issues between the bishop and me."

It had been reported earlier that Bishop Myers apparently favors erecting a high-rise retirement home on the grounds of Grace Cathedral. The tax-free income from the development would be a considerable boon to the diocese.

The dispute was said to center over whether administration of the cathedral's $9.5 million worth of property on Nob Hill and its $500,000 treasury should be controlled by the diocesan office.

Flux

Dean Bartlett attributed his difficulties to "a breakdown of communications."

"The situation is in a state of flux," he said. "I am sure the bishop is as desirous of reestablishing communication with me as I am to reestablish communication with him."

Dean Bartlett said that because of the fluid nature of the situation he thought "it would be inappropriate if not in bad taste to discuss the situation in any detail . . ."

He said "some dimensions of what is happening are highly personal in nature and therefore would be inappropriate for public discussion."

Control

Myers had been quoted as saying the transfer of control of Grace Cathedral's finances to the diocese would be "the happy

by-product of freeing the dean from all administrative responsibilities."

He also said Bartlett's resignation would allow the dean to
"apply his enormous creative abilities to the ecclesiastical and
community demands of his office."

Myers said he would bring up the question of Dean Bartlett's
removal at a meeting of the Grace Cathedral board of trustees
in the fall.

Dean Bartlett could be removed from his post only by a majority vote of the trustees, and only after "grave cause" had been
established. [4]

The term *power* perhaps more than any other sums up both
the problems and the promises of the modern world. Never
has man had so much power—physical, technological, organizational—at his disposal. And never has man been so perplexed
as to how he may harness this enormous potential for creative ends without being destroyed by it. The Greeks, of course,
felt some of the same ambivalence, symbolically represented by fire. The discovery of fire was regarded as a benefit to
man; and yet, as Aeschylus dramatizes it, Prometheus in bringing down fire to his fellows in defiance of the Olympian gods
becomes not just a heroic benefactor but a condemned crim-
inal chained to the mountains with vultures eating his insides
out.

The dilemma remains the same, though the dimensions
of the drama have been enormously magnified. In contemporary society every institution, public and private, is faced with
the problem of employing the expanded power available in
such a way that it is not self-destructive. That is, there is a growing recognition that power must be exercized with humility
and that to be defiant of the destructive potentialities of its
"heat" is to invite the judgment of the gods.

With the increased size and complexity of society, political
institutions in particular are being put to the test as to whether
increased governmental power now held or potentially available may not become the cause of their own downfall. There
is a growing awareness that, unless these institutions—among

them the church—find the forms and processes that can cope with the forces unleashed by the technological revolution, they are threatened with extinction.

The new science of cybernetics is one reponse to this crisis. The father of cybernetics, Norbert Wiener, describes how through "feedback" a system may be engineered to have those qualities of adaptability and flexibility which will enable it to survive and function effectively in response to the demands placed upon it, including those forces which the system itself has generated: "Feedback is a method of controlling a system by reinserting into it the results of its past performance. . . . If the information which proceeds backward from the performance is able to change the general method and pattern of performance, we have a process which may well be called learning."[5]

If the church, and its political forms and processes in particular, is viewed as such a system, it is clear that it is finding great difficulty in learning, in Wiener's sense, how to facilitate a feedback of its own performance and thus bring about a change in its methods and patterns. One can see that, not only in the general cultural milieu but also within its own life, the church has been the source of many of the political ideals which have shaped modern life and institutions. Contemporary corporate structures and procedures as well as many of the powerful ideological currents of democracy may be traced back to Christian origins. But how can they be fed back into the ecclesiastical system?

The Roman Catholic Church is implicated in this revolution in two ways. In the first place, it is one of those traditional institutions whose ideology, constitution, and political processes seem to have been overrun by modern technological culture. The sharpness of the popular reaction within the Catholic Church against the Pope's encyclical on birth control, as well as the extent of the resistance to its directives, is partly explainable in terms of a feeling, especially among the well-educated laity, that the ethical principles outlined were not sufficiently informed by modern technological advances in biological and chemical science, making many of the encyclical's basic assumptions about marriage and procreation obsolete.

In the second place, the authority of the encyclical was undermined by the widespread suspicion among the clergy that reactionaries in the Curia were principally responsible for the main ideological thrusts of the document. The Pope's statement was thus seen, rightly or wrongly, as one which documented a great ideological power struggle within the Roman Church and was, therefore, given a "party" label. Thus it lacked authoritative power in circles antagonistic to the party position it symbolically represented, that is, the position of the "small power group," which, as Hans Küng termed it, was "backward-looking, ghetto-bound and unecumenical, both traditionalist and nationalist in its thinking."[6] The encyclical, insofar as it was seen as a symbol of the power struggle within the Roman Catholic Church, was particularly threatening to the liberal factions because it seemed to indicate that the Pope was succumbing to political pressures from the Curia and was, by implication, giving up his intention stated previously (in his address to the Curia on September 21, 1963) of prodding "the Curia itself [to] take the lead in that process of renewal which is constantly necessary in the Church as a human and earthly institution."[7]

But Protestantism is also profoundly affected by the same ideological and political currents. On the purely institutional side, Protestantism is in many ways more traumatized by the modern organizational revolution than Catholicism. In some ways Roman Catholicism's structure is more adaptable to the size and complexity of modern society with its combination of central ideological authority and decentralized administrative authority through the episcopal system. Protestantism, on the other hand, with its traditional emphasis on individual authority and decentralized polity, finds the exigencies of modern centralized bureaucratic controls and ideological direction both psychologically distasteful and theologically threatening. More than for Roman Catholicism, Protestantism is inclined to view Bigness as Badness. Some of the reaction against the large-scale denominational as well as ecumenical ecclesiastical organizations is not only a sign of a younger generation's anti-institutional bias but also a deep backlash arising out of Protestantism's past fears and reservations about centralized church power and nondemocratic church government.

But Protestantism is also being shaken from within by political forces. Members of the younger generation are demanding more political representation in the policy-making and decision-making boards and committees in many Protestant churches and are making it evident, whether at World Council of Churches assemblies, or in theological seminaries, or in local congregations, that they will not be satisfied with less than a real share in the political power within the life of the church.

Also, minority groups are demanding greater political voice in the affairs of their churches and in many cases are already wielding effective political power. For example, such political-action groups as the various all-black caucuses—Black Unitarians for Radical Reform in Los Angeles, Alamo Black Clergy in Oakland, the National Committee of Black Churchmen—are, as one caucus leader put it, "simply the banding together of black people in the church to goad the church fathers to do the things they'd already promised to do. . . . The caucus is a responsible manifestation of Black Power."[8] It is evident that segregated church headquarters and racial discrimination practiced on fellow bishops by ecclesiastical functionaries is going to meet more than mild verbal protests in the future, whether in Protestant or Catholic provinces.

Radical political dysfunctioning can lead to equally radical political despair, whether in an institution or in the state, and is a strong invitation to political cynicism and apathy. But this does not seem to be the predominant response of the present generation. Action rather than drop-out seems to be the major response. In this sense the struggle of a writer such as Ignazio Silone, through his novels, with the "central dilem-

ma of all political action: the only certain way of preventing
bureaucracy is to refrain from organization, but the refusal
to organize with one's fellow men can lead only to acquiescence in detested power, or to isolated and futile acts of mar-
tyrdom and terrorism,"[9] resonates in all churches today.

In this, as well as in the cases cited at the beginning of this
chapter, it is evident that the problem of the distribution and
control of power is constant and universal in church life. This
is particularly awkward for an association which in so many
respects in its ethical position appears to be inviting men to
a life based on the renunciation of power. Newton Flew's study
of *The Idea of Perfection* is one of the fairest analyses of the
history of Christian attempts to reconcile the apparently ab-
solutist ethic of nonresistance and pacifism—the denial of
power in the name of religion—and the hard realities of individual and social life in which the possession and exercise
of power is a *sine qua non* of existence. Many of the most important chapters in the history of the development of Christian ethical theory are focused on this issue.

If the injunction "You therefore must be perfect, as your
heavenly Father is perfect" is taken as one of the foundation
stones of Christian ethics, it is clear that those thinkers and
movements that have identified themselves most strongly with
the motif of perfection in their ethical theory, and have made
it central in their systems, have tended to deal with the reality of power largely in a negative way. The ideal of perfection
has been associated with such divine attributes as love and
holiness. God as power, however, has not, on the whole, provided a similar model for ethical perfection. To seek to approximate the perfect love of God has been a vitalizing idea
in the history of Christian ethics; the idea of seeking to approximate God's power has had no such impact.

But in considering church politics, the issue of power cannot be evaded. Power is an intrinsic element in the politics
of the church, as it is in all other political existence. Unless
power is recognized, political theory becomes hallucinatory and
political action becomes irresponsible and eventually anarchic.

Bertrand de Jouvenel writes: "The differences between forms of government in different societies and the changes of form within the same society are but the accidents, to borrow the terminology of philosophy, of the same essence. . . . The discussion of the different forms of Power is always with us because, there being in every society a centre of control, everyone is naturally interested in the questions of its powers, its organization, and its conduct."[10] Or, as Bertrand Russell puts it: "the fundamental concept in social science is Power, in the same sense in which Energy is the fundamental concept in physics. . . . The laws of social dynamics are . . . only capable of being stated in terms of power in its various forms."[11]

The question then is: When one considers church politics, can piety and power be reconciled in the Christian context? Christian theologians and moralists have generally found it more difficult to appropriate the divine attribute of power in relation to individual life or social reality than love and holiness. This has been true in all of the major Christian traditions.

Reinhold Neibuhr confirms this in his assessment of the present religious ethos of the churches. On one side, popular piety is strongly conditioned by ascetic and mystic influences, with their stress on the theme of holiness. "The essential mark of Pietism is its quest for individual holiness."[12] the other side, the more sophisticated theological mainstream in both Catholicism and Protestantism has tended to concentrate on the theme of love. Niebuhr says, "Catholic thought . . . in its classical version . . . is more inclined than the Reformation to interpret love as *pleroma* of everything intended in nature and in law." Nevertheless, it is also true that "modern liberal Protestantism is inclined to equate law and love by its effort to comprehend all law within the love commandment."[13]

It is always precarious to make generalizations about amorphous realities such as "popular piety" or "folk religiosity." However, recognizing the necessarily "popular" character of politics, it is probably at this level that the conflict between piety and the idea of power is most accentuated. For if the concepts of love and holiness have in fact been predominant in the shaping of Western Christian piety, as seems to be the case, it is obvious that power does not fit easily into the conceptual categories of that mentality. Thus, even the *idea* of church politics itself, understood in power terms, becomes difficult to accept and assimilate. Furthermore, at the popular level the religious orientation of popular piety, directed by the themes of love and holiness, is bolstered by the romanticism and optimism of secular Liberalism. Religious perfectionism and sociological utopianism become intermeshed. The romantic ideals of purity and love become interwoven with Christian beliefs about holiness and charity.

It is this complex world-view, both in regard to oneself and to the external environment, that makes up popular piety—and its vitality as well as its persistence owes much to the variety of factors that constitute it. It is strong because it has so many supportive secular connections. It is deep because it is so closely identified with the profound levels of religious conviction and response. Furthermore, the fact that it functions at both the conscious and the unconscious levels means that it is not diverted by argumentation on the basis of simple, rational logic, nor is it fundamentally altered by simple theological appeals.

In many areas of life the positive contribution of power is taken for granted, whether it is the horsepower of the vehicle that transports or the economic power of the money that provides necessities as well as luxuries. In business and in politics power is sought, used, and admired. Yet, popular religious piety still seems to avoid coming to terms with the fact of power. It is rationalized, or romanticized, or relegated to the sphere of the secular, which, in this outlook is separate from the "religious" realm and is, therefore, "unspiritual" in any case. Power is considered part of that untamed, brutish element of life which is unredeemed—however necessary it may be for survival—and about which one has certain undefined but actual guilt feelings, especially acute because one in reality is so dependent upon power for one's survival and welfare.

Thus it is not surprising that within the church the reality of power becomes so difficult to admit, so awkward to handle. It is rejected. It is disguised. It is explained away. But it stubbornly remains. Formally exorcised, it sinks beneath the surface, occasionally erupting in a chaotic way, and, in a subterranean fashion, persistently and destructively undermining the order of the church. Denied recognition, power is also by the same token denied the rational correctives of theological criticism as well as the spiritual disciplines of authentic piety whereby it might be channeled in a constructive way for the edification of the communal structures and the common life. For social power which is not politically ordered inevitably becomes the force of anarchy: social dissolution, personal demoralization, institutional deterioration follow in course. If the modern church is sick, this may well be one of the major causes of its malaise: the repression of power.

Political reform and renewal are always dependent on ideological and "spiritual" factors. As Lenin, the master tactician of revolution, wrote in his tract *What Is to Be Done? Burning Questions of our Movement*: "Without a revolutionary theory there can be no revolutionary movement."[14] Lenin elsewhere describes what it means to "learn" the theory: it does not consist, he tells young Communists, solely in "imbibing the sum of knowledge that is contained in communist text-books, pamphlets, and books. . . . such a definition of the study of Communism would be too crude and inadequate. . . ." He continues: "It would be still more dangerous to start to imbibe only communist slogans." The fact is, he asserts, that the constructive work of building a new society can be undertaken "only by mastering all modern knowledge, only if you are able to transform Communism from ready-made, memorized formulas, counsels, recipes, prescriptions and programs into that living thing which unites your immediate work, and only if you are able to transform Communism into a guide for your practical work."[15]

This digestion of doctrine into a "living thing," this inner appropriation of the theory which transforms into a "guide" for work and a unitive power for action, could be called a description of the dynamics of piety. A distinction should be made, therefore, between true and false piety, or between *piety* and *pietism*. For authentic piety, the depth assimilation of dogma, is the root source of response and action, whether it be in Communism or in Christianity. It must, as Lenin suggests, be unitive: that is, it must bring faith and action together so that action is a reflection of faith, and faith is consistent with action. It must also have integrity: that is, it must possess an inner consistency so that essentially contradictory ideals do not negate one another and lead to impotency. Finally, it must be comprehensive: that is, it involves "mastering all modern knowledge" so that every aspect of experience and understanding is incorporated within it and thus it does not result in schizophrenic paralysis or hallucinatory escapism. True piety, then, is not something apart from the world. It illuminates the real world, and the real world is illuminated by it.

In this light, the meaning of the injunction "you must be perfect" takes on a different complexion. For it suggests that true piety is authenticated by its integrity and wholeness. It is not hypocritical: there is no play-acting, no dissimulation, no essential discrepancy between the various elements of faith. It is not dualistic: there is no contradiction between the commitments of faith and the commitments of action. It is not atomistic: it is one thing through and through.

What is required for healthy church politics is an assimilation in its piety of the reality of its politics. If power is an intrinsic ingredient in politics then the reality of power has to be constitutively incorporated in church piety. Otherwise, church politics becomes, quite literally, schizophrenic. If this synthesis does not take place either the politics or the piety is falsified, or both.

To reform the politics of the church, therefore, means in the first place a dogmatic redefinition of piety. Only in this way can its piety be reality oriented rather than wish oriented, to use psychological terminology. The church's piety should not only incorporate ought-ness but is-ness. Spiritual health, like mental health, is marked by the ability to reconcile was-ness, is-ness, and ought-ness—past, present, and future

—in a harmonious and dynamic synthesis. Politics is centered on the *now,* it is concerned with is-ness (though was-ness and ought-ness—history and hope—are also its concern), and a piety which is relevant to politics is one in which is-ness is also central.

The dogmatic restructuring of the church's piety to make it politically relevant means, for example, an appropriation in piety of the dogmatic faith that "you would have no power . . . unless it had been given you from above" (John 19:11), "for there is no power but of God" (Rom. 13:1). This dogmatic principle is next theologically paraphrased and interpreted; as for instance in the following exposition of Paul Tillich: "Present-day physics speaks of power-fields in order to describe the basic structures of the material world. This is at least an indication of the significance the term 'power' has even in the most abstract analysis of physical occurrences. . . . We must ask, how is it possible that both physics and social science use the same word, 'power'? There must be a point of identity between the structure of the social and the structure of the physical world. And this identity must be manifest in the common use of the term 'power'. There is, however, only one way of discovering the root meaning of power, namely to ask about its ontological foundation." Tillich goes on to distinguish between physical power (force) and psychological power (compulsion) and asks whether there is not a third kind of power— spiritual. This is divine power, in which, and in which alone, all the forms of power are united. Metaphorically applied to man, it may then be generally said: "Being is the power of being! . . . the dynamic self-affirmation of life overcoming internal and external resistance. . . . Non-being is the negation of being within being itself. . . . The self-affirmation of a being is correlate to the power of being it embodies. It is greater in man than in animals and in some men greater than others. A life process is the more powerful, the more non-being it can include in its self-affirmation, without being destroyed by it. The neurotic can include only a little non-being, the average man a limited amount, the creative man a large amount, God—symbolically speaking—an infinite amount. The self-affirmation of being in spite of non-being is the expression of its power of being. Here we are at the roots of the concept of power. Power is the possibility of self-affirmation in spite of internal and external negation. It is the possibility of overcoming non-being. Human power is the possibility of man to overcome non-being infinitely."[16]

Such a theological interpretation is then appropriated in piety. Prayed in both heart and mind, the "kingdom and the power and the glory" becomes words with content, verbal signs of an inner affirmation—an "amen"—to power as part of the description of the ultimate structure of reality. Political theory and political action become spontaneous depth expressions through theological rationality and spiritual piety of this ultimate dogmatic truth about the ontological source of power.

Both reason and faith are appropriately employed in the formulation of political theory and in the engagement in political action. Policy as well as participation are conditioned by both reason and faith. In church politics it is particularly important to stress this point. Because the church is often considered, consciously and unconsciously, to be the domain of "mystery" (and this is often understood in a magical and superstitious way), the church may be recognized as a "power structure," but yet that power is denied the rational controls of logical analysis as well as the qualifying conditioning of theological insight and spiritual sensitivity. In a practical sense, this leads to apathy or cynicism.

In order to clarify the relevance of this generalization for church politics, the relation of reason to the structures of the church and the relation of faith to its processes should be considered.

In what way might reason be considered the guiding principle in assessing the polities of the church? The Case of the Methodist Publishing House was a "shocker" for the delegates of the General Conference. But why? According to the reporter, it was presumably the disclosure of the discrepancy between the salary of the president of the church's publishing house and those of the bishops. In an institution ostensibly committed to a faith which has had as one of its characteristic ideals the model of poverty exhibited by its founder and which at least formally has taught that, though "the love of money is the root of all evil," the charitable and benevolent use of financial power is the commendable form of Christian service, the salaries of the bishops themselves might be considered a "sensation." The point of the story, however, is that the *discrepancy* between the salaries becomes sensational. One might look on this as a somewhat distorted expression of the ideal of equality for the Christian community—distorted because it seems to be interpreted in terms of the expectation of equal affluence rather than common poverty.

But there may be a more fundamental reason for the sense of scandal. Money is popularly recognized as a form of power. Salaries in this instance are symbolic of power, and differences in salaries symbolic of hierarchical differentials in the power structure. But is this not a very "secular" way of looking at the church? Precisely. And this is in part the reason for the feeling of shock on the part of the delegates. In the secular sphere, they are acquainted with this symbolic identification of money with power. Subconsciously, they apply the same analysis to the financial structure of the church. But the power structure that it symbolizes does not correspond with the formal structure articulated in its polity. According to one value system, the president of the publishing house is supreme in power. In the other value system, the bishops prevail. Which evaluation is correct? Which is right?

This poses the political problem. It appears on first glance that the Case of the Methodist Publishing House raises a moral question and that is all. But viewed in political terms, the moral issue becomes more complex. It involves the problem of power. Ethically speaking, power is neutral. Theologically, as has been seen, it is essentially positive. Politically, it is ambiguous. The critical problem is, then, how to politically rationalize the power structure of the church. That is, how can the formal polity—the constitutional description of the theoretical power structure—be brought into harmony with the real power structure of the church?

In this particular case, one solution would be to assign salaries on the basis of the formal structure of polity. The bishops would get more and the publishing house president less. But it may be that, functionally speaking, the office of the publishing house president *is* more important than the office of bishop—as a power structure, the church may in fact be more dependent on the effective functioning of the publishing house than on the competency of the bishops. Furthermore, if the essential functions of the episcopate are dynamically interpreted, and not formalistically, and apostolic succession is treated as functional continuity rather than formal historical continuation (the perpetuation of the "Gothic spirit" over against the preservation of the "Gothic style," to refer to Frank Lloyd Wright again), it may be that the administrator of the publishing house is a new form of episcopacy. The president of the central communications center of the church is, in a transformed way, fulfilling the teaching function of the episcopate. Thus, politically speaking, could he not be viewed as a successor to the apostles, a traditional bishop in bureaucratic disguise? The political problem is, then, putting aside the specific moral question of the proper relation of salary and status, to reconcile the different value systems operating in the church and, most importantly, to restructure rationally the polity (including the assignment of appropriate titles for the offices) so that form does follow function.

The Protestant tradition has been marked by its emphasis on the principle "by faith alone." There is, however, a corollary to it: "by reason alone." Arguing the case of Christian freedom for the ordering of the structural and organizational life of the church, Luther maintains that though St. Paul's exhortation "All things should be done decently and in order" (1 Cor. 14:40) is valid, this must be realized in freedom. In fact, it is only when it is interpreted in a spirit of freedom that it becomes a viable principle of order. And to use the precept as a guide and criterion for the ordering of the church's life requires the use of reason. It is, in short, a rational principle. Church offices, sacramental signs, ecclesiastical vestments, liturgical forms, and organizational arrangements are intended to be, says Luther, "tolerable, kind, and pleasant means" through which God does his work. Such "external signs and holy possessions" are not intended to become burdensome. Rather, they are functional means to the end that the church, the Christian community, should be enabled "in love and friendliness" to worship God and serve the neighbor. If, however, the means becomes the end in itself—as Luther believed the case to be with canon law—then it must be corrected or abolished. In other words, church order should be an expression of Christian liberty, not a denial of it.[17]

All these "externals"—everything from set times for services to church buildings, from sacramental elements to church law—"house, altar, pulpit, baptismal font, candlesticks, candles, bells, priestly vestments, and the like"—are a part of the natural ordering of man's life and thus "these things have no more than their natural effects." The realm of church order is, therefore, a dimension of secular reality. Consequently, when Luther says in his characteristically paradoxical way that "God, Christ, and the Holy Spirit are not interested in them" he is not projecting an ontological dualism but is, with poetic exaggeration, making a distinction between direct divine jurisdiction of the church and indirect, instrumental government. It is in this instrumental fashion that divine politics is effective. This is true, says Luther, in all the "three hierarchies ordained by God"—home, state, church; in each case, "the Holy Spirit reigns there," not in a direct manner, but instrumentally in a "natural" and "temporal" mode.

In this sense, human rationality is a beneficial expression of, and a useful gift from, the Holy Spirit for man's ordering of his common life in the world. Metaphorically speaking, it is proper to "regard these externals as we do a christening robe or swaddling clothes." At baptism the external coverings are not needed, "and yet reason dictates that a child be thus clothed."

This appeal to the "dictates of reason" as the criteria for church order does not imply—as it was misinterpreted by some Lutheran moralists in regard to political ethics—the relegation of the secular sphere to pure chance, or the abandonment of the secular to the whims of fortune. It is again the elevation of the pragmatic and functional considerations to an ethical position. Prudence and "moderation" become critical factors in determining what institutional and governmental forms are needed and how they are to be used in the church. To be a wise "politician" in the church means thus, as Luther puts it, to "exercise moderation and not use too many of these garments, lest the child be smothered."

Luther articulates this functional principle for the political ordering of the church in this succinct way: whether it be in respect to ceremonies, or institutions, or organizational structures, "They must remain so light that they are not felt." The use of power is thereby qualified and conditioned by the exercise of reason. So, both reason and power are positively affirmed as pneumatological instrumentalities. They are both rooted in the same ontological matrix: God's providential care for the world. In a particular way, consequently, it may be asserted: "These matters are purely external (as far as time, place, and persons are concerned) and may be *regulated entirely by reason, to which they are entirely subject.*" In a general way, power is to be disciplined and regulated by rationality; it is to be "entirely subject" to the moderating government of reason and it is by reason and "by reason alone" that it is to be controlled.[18]

It may be that the belief that reason can curb power is too sanguine to eventuate in an ethic which can realistically cope with the irrational elements in man's behavior or come to terms with the relativities and complexities of political conflict. Nevertheless, even accepting these reservations, the assignment to reason of the dominating role in determining the order of the church and in the political regulation of its life has at least the negative merit of removing church politics from the sphere of magic and mysticism. This principle at least has the virtue

of demystifying ecclesiastical life and of forcing a consideration of the dilemmas of church politics at the level of rational
reflection rather than emotional reaction.

Positively, "reason," interpreted in the broadest sense as
representing the totality of man's natural intelligence and mental capabilities, is a principle which is conducive to functional
and pragmatic approaches to the ordering of the life of the
church. The appeal to rational control of power should stimulate creativity—through "architectural imagination" or "political wit"—in attacking the institutional and organizational
problems of the church. Church politics thereby would not
be intimidated by the "holiness" of the church, magically conceived. Rationality cuts through all such mystiques, and bol-
sters man's self-confidence in dealing with the technical as
well as the emotional factors which are shaping the corporate existence of the Christian body. The political dynamics
of the church should not be inhibited by the otherworldly and
anti-incarnational assumptions about the peculiar, "spiritual"
character of the ecclesiastical community. On the basis of the
principle "by reason alone," the politics of the church can be
renewed and its institutions reformed, for the church is no
longer considered as a "totem" object, but a sacrament whose
elements are natural; whose power is not a taboo force but
a divinely derived source of its vitality which is to be construc-
tively ordered for the general welfare. Civil politics has to do
with the *structure of power*. It has also to do with the *balance
of power*. This is also true of church politics. In regard to the
balance of power, we are dealing with a dynamic category
as distinct from a formal one, as in the case of power *structure*. The rational principle is not irrelevant to questions having to do with the balance of power, because dynamics are
structured. Power is itself a dynamic reality, though it assumes
structured forms. The political term "dynasty" carries in it this
double entendre. If reason is understood to incorporate such
qualities as imagination and ingenuity, it is obviously not irrelevant to the more dynamic aspects of power structure.

Nevertheless, insofar as power balance is more oriented

toward political process than toward political form, the category of faith may be more appropriate to this political dimension than reason. Because faith is a "depth" category, it may more closely correspond to the depth elements involved in the balance of power. Furthermore, since the balance of power has to do in part with the tensions induced by conflicting *claims,* the belief element in faith has a certain correspondence with it. Finally, faith as a quality may approximate the harmonious tension implied in the integration of conflicting claims through the realization of a balance of power.

To be more specific: conflict is characteristic of politics. This conflict may arise from the confrontation between rival interests. Even more profoundly, however, political conflict is rooted in the depths of faith, that is, in the fundamental opposition of rival faiths, in the basic beliefs about the ultimate nature of things, about what is finally "the true, the good, and the beautiful." To balance the power of the rival interests is largely a formal matter, the realization of which puts a premium on rational ingenuity. To balance the power of rival faiths, on the other hand, requires the power of faith itself. Because faith is ultimate commitment, "faith alone" and not reason is capable of transcending faith.

This is, of course, where all politics becomes "sticky" but pre-eminent in the church as a "community of faith." The conflicting claims of rival faiths cannot be harmonized "by reason alone." To the extent that these faiths represent, in Tillich's term, "ultimate concern," they cannot be simply formally reconciled at a rational level in an external structure of power. Only a dynamic *balance* offers the potentialities for this depth kind of reconciliation and integration.

Failure to recognize this depth character of political conflict and failure to understand the dynamics of faith involved often sours church politics. For to realize a balance of power within the community of faith means to effect a consensus of faith. Only a common faith can transcend the conflicts invoked by depth confrontation between rival faiths.

This seems simple enough. But is it? The balance of power

in the realm of faith cannot be achieved by superficial, syncretistic harmonization. Nor can it be realized by a sentimental consensus. In neither case is the "depth" character of faith conflict recognized. It is here that the ontological character of faith must be discerned. Ironically, it appears that conflict is intrinsic to the ontology of faith. It has an essential polarity and its "balance" is realized through the opposition of counterforces, not through their resolution.

To be more explicit: affirmation is characteristic of faith. Because faith is personal this inevitably implies self-affirmation. Self-affirmation must be balanced by the affirmation of others, and this means an inevitable conflict between different self-affirmations. Since love and justice cannot be separated from faith, such self-affirmations cannot be "faithfully" expressed at the expense of other "faithful" self-affirmations. The Christian believer, in particular, is called upon to love his neighbor as himself. His faith does not allow him to love himself to the detriment of his neighbor. But neither does his faith, as legitimate self-affirmation, allow him to affirm his neighbor to the extent of denying his own being. Self-love, in this sense, and the love of others must be in a "balance of power." This suggests ambiguities, for this basic conflict cannot be resolved without denying one's own being or the being of the other. As Tillich puts it: "Spiritual power is not the conquest of these ambiguities but resignation of power, because this would mean resignation of being. It would be the attempt to annihilate oneself in order to escape guilt." In the last analysis, Tillich concludes, "Spiritual power is not the denial of power dynamics."[19] In other words, life as a totality is a balance of power. And in order to be true to life, this must be accepted and not denied.

This is a familiar phenomenon seen from the perspective of modern physics, which is more and more viewing the ultimate reality of things not in structural terms or in harmonization, but in dynamic terms and in polarization. One research physicist has stated that nouns are passé in modern physics;

only verbs will do. Likewise, therefore, in the realm of faith the balance of power can be seen as a dynamic tension whose realization is dependent on the recognition of the essential "conflict" ontologically characteristic of the very nature of existence as such.

Applied to church politics and the question of balance of power, conflict appears to be instrinsic, not only to politics, but to the whole of existence. Thus a political balance of power is to be visualized not as a resolution of conflict, into peaceful harmony, or a reduction of conflict into static consensus, but a vital and creative polarization in which conflict is recognized as the essential mark of life itself. To deny conflict in church politics may be not only politically unrealistic but actually a form of ontological heresy!

Anthony Storrs, a leading British psychoanalyst, asserts that "aggression is a drive as innate, as natural, and as powerful as sex. . . . in man, as in other animals, the aggressive drive is an inherited constant, of which we cannot rid ourselves, and which is absolutely necessary for survival." Storrs also affirms that "disagreement, controversy, and even competitive striving have a positive function in human existence," particularly in defining personal identity: "For how can a man know who he is, and what he thinks and believes, unless there are others who think and believe differently? In life it is essential that we come up against other people or we cease to exist as individuals. . . . The maintenance of human identity requires opposition."[20] Storrs points out that the various circles of experts in psychology have had difficulty in coming to a common mind on the sources, meaning, and potentialities of the aggressive component in human nature.

If this deep-seated ambivalence toward aggression—power personally embodied—exists among those most intimately acquainted with its manifestation in individual men and women, it is not surprising that within the church "the aggressive component" finds difficulty in gaining recognition as having a positive function for the individual, but more particularly, in the political life of the community. The Case of the Bishop and the Dean illustrates the tensions which are created by power conflicts in the church, especially those which involve "disagreement, controversy, and even competitive striving" between respected authority figures in the religious fellowship.

It is evident in this specific case that the conflict arises in part over juridical and constitutional questions involving disagreement not only about what the intrinsic powers of a bishop and a dean are but also disagreement about the separation of these powers vis-à-vis one another. In this particular situation, the powers appear to overlap. In a sense, this is strictly a legal question. It amounts to differences of interpretation of what the polity says, representing variant readings of the nature of the power structure. They also represent different understandings of both the limitations of power and the extent of power of two related offices.

Such definitions of the limits and extent of power are most difficult to determine at the second level of command in an organization. Though it is not strictly accurate as an analogy, the difficulties which business corporations have experienced in defining the status and function of the "vice-president" echelons in their hierarchy somewhat parallels the difficulties which ecclesiastical bodies have in defining the roles of their "v.p.'s"— whether it be a cathedral dean over against a bishop, or a cardinal over against the pope, or an assistant pastor over against the head minister.[21] Thus to infer that the essential issue can be resolved by describing the conflict as just a case of "standard business procedure" is really not only to fail to appreciate the underlying issue relating to the basic power structure of the church but also indicates a lack of realism about the moral and political complexities inherent in business procedure itself. As one guide for management has it: "Business is not nice, and it is an illusion to try to make it nice; so long as the fruit of dynamic progress is desired—and by desired we do not necessarily mean desirable in religious or philosophical terms—its price must be paid."[22]

"Nice" should be understood in the sense that there is a

certain roughness in corporate processes. This is intrinsic to the enterprise, for dynamic change challenges the "nice" structural rigidities that hinder transition, and the powers involved are too potent (the dynamics of a body are proportional to the powers that it incorporates) to be neatly restricted to "nice" structural arrangements. "Nice" in this context is a descriptive rather than an ethical term. But even in the business community, popular moral sensibilities are often offended by the necessities of corporate existence. Thus, the prestige of the big business executive is somehow tainted by the suspicion of the public that his status is achieved and his power exercised without observing normal, accepted "niceties." As John Kenneth Galbraith observes: "Although in his hierarchical role in the large corporation he has, perhaps, been more successful than most in eliminating economic insecurity, both personal and institutional, he has even managed to retain a certain cachet as a risk-taker, a man who lives dangerously."[23] Therefore, as another management analyst puts it: "They work in secret. . . and they have a shrewd suspicion that the less the public sees and hears of them in the flesh, the better they get along."[24]

These "nice" moral sensibilities and expectations of the public complicate the corporate politics of the church even more than they do those of secular corporations. Church officers, especially those whose role is closely connected with symbolic functions surrounding a "public image," such as a bishop, are deprived of the opportunity of carrying on their executive responsibilities in complete privacy. They cannot "work in secret" when their symbolic functions demand public exposure. One suspects, however, whether in secular institutions or in religious, that the secrecy which executive life seems to invite is not intrinsic to it but is imposed by the sentimental moral "niceties" of the public and by popular unwillingness to accept conflict as an indispensable factor in dynamic creativity and the refusal to admit power as a constructive potentiality in life.

To achieve a *balance* of power in the Case of the Bishop and the Dean, outside of the legal issues related to the power

structure, is extraordinarily difficult. The concern for respect-
ing the "honor and integrity" of the parties involved is authentic, not only in the sense of explicit moral rightness in so doing
but also implicitly in the acknowledgement of the "public"
role of these officials and the symbolic significance attached
to them. In ordinary politics it is often possible to distinguish
"person" and "office"; but in the church this cannot so easily
be accomplished—for some of the reasons already mentioned.
Nevertheless, it is clear that the public dispute, and the reports
of it, "did not treat the main issues between the bishop and
me," as the dean put it. What these are is not exactly stated
but it is evident, as the dean says, "some dimensions of what
is happening are highly personal in nature and therefore would
be inappropriate for public discussion."

But this raises a "nice" point. If it is because of "the fluid
nature of the situation," as the report has it, that it is considered "inappropriate if not in bad taste to discuss the situation
in any detail" there is a certain plausibility to the argument.
For there are certain circumstances in politics in which the
fluidity of the situation makes the balancing of power a very
delicate operation—in volatile diplomatic negotiations, for
example—and in which public disclosure of the process might
introduce other power factors into the equation which would
incalculably complicate the problem of realizing a balance.
But if, on the other hand, the *sole* reason for insisting on the
inappropriateness of public discussion is that the issues are
basically "highly personal in nature," then the argument is
invalid. For the bishop and the dean, whether they like it or
not, are also highly *public* in nature. The issues between them,
therefore, are inevitably also highly public in nature.

The fact that the dispute has become public property through
the news media proves that. Public discussion may be inappropriate, it may even be in "bad taste," but it is unavoidable.
The "breakdown in communications" is not only one between
the bishop and the dean, therefore, but between the "power
elite" of the church and its constituency and, perhaps also,
in a deeper sense, between the church and the world, between

the pulpit and the press. The public is confused and the news reports mirror that confusion (though the reporter himself is an ecclesiastically ordained functionary and "insider," who thus shows greater insight into the nuances of the conflict than a complete outsider.

In any case, the dispute becomes scandalous not because of the heat but because of the humility! That is, the rising temperatures are generated by the power dynamics operating. But the heat becomes oppressive when it has inadequate outlets. Thus again, it is not the fact of power but the denial of power that is politically destructive. The public does not understand the dispute. They impose on their church leaders a style of "humility" which does not allow them to be honest about the power dilemma they are facing, or candid about all the factors, "personal" or otherwise, which are generating the political heat.

Humility of this kind is highly ambivalent in its political potentialities. Humility understood as the recognition of another's rights is a moderating influence in political conflict. But humility understood as total self-negation becomes politically irresponsible. It is, as has been said, ontologically heretical, for it refuses to acknowledge power as a part of is-ness and this culminates in the political sphere in all sorts of practical falsifications. In brief: theological errancy leads to political dishonesty, theological disintegration to political disintegration. As Niebuhr says: "In one sense the presence or absence of cynicism among the oligarchs is beside the point. The important point is that ruthless power operates behind a screen of pretended ideal ends, a situation which is both more dangerous and more evil than pure cynical defiance of moral ends. It corresponds to the weakness of the human heart more nearly than absolute cynicism, for men are less inclined to pure cynicism than to the delusion that they serve some noble purpose in engaging in projects which serve their own end."[25]

There is considerable historical evidence to substantiate this thesis. Bertrand Russell chronicles this in the medieval church. He says that the greatest strength of the church was "the moral respect which it inspired." It inherited "as a kind of moral capital" the glory of the persecutions, the impressive austerity and sacrificial character of celibacy, the holiness of the saints—all of which "dazzled public opinion." Ironically, as Russell sees it, precisely this popular piety authentically evoked by the church prevented popular moral pressures from correcting the church in its aberrancies: the poverty of the friars so impressed the world that it gave the money to make the church wealthy, the world-negating spirit of the monastic life bolstered the popular support of the church to the extent that it became supreme over monarchs, the preaching of brotherly love by St. Francis "generated the enthusiasm required for the victorious prosecution of a long and atrocious war. In the end, the Renaissance Church lost all the moral purpose to which it owed its wealth and power, and the shock of the Reformation was necessary to produce regeneration." Thus, concludes Russell: "to an organization which has ideal ends, and therefore an excuse for love of power, a reputation for superior virtue is dangerous, and is sure, in the long run, to produce a superiority only in unscrupulous ruthlessness."[26]

The theological self-image of the church must incorporate within it the reality of the church as a power complex. Its piety must appropriate this self-image and, at the same time, assimilate the concomitant theological affirmation of the positive nature of power. Only then can the practical issues of conflict in the church be dealt with in realistic humility. It is with humility insofar as it recognizes the limitations of human nature and the ultimate source of power. It is with realism insofar as it recognizes the reality of power and the conflict inherent in man's existence and the ultimate nature of things. This is the base on which creative church politics can be grounded and constructed.

As has been suggested, the political difficulties which the church has in ordering its organizational life are not simply the fault of the church leaders. Reinhold Niebuhr rightly notes that it is well to be aware of "the dangers in the pretensions of wisdom and disinterestedness which are made by an elite."[27] But one of the reasons why it may be necessary for a church politician to engage in this type of pretentiousness, even if it is personally distasteful to him, is that the popular spiritual ethos of the church community does not allow place for the legitimate exercise of political power, does not tolerate the overt demonstration of aggressive competition or controversy within its fellowship. The power, coercive or otherwise, which is necessary to maintain corporate political life must, therefore, be repressed or camouflaged, and, in that disguised form, theologically rationalized.

Niebuhr cites the medieval papacy in this connection: "The structure of power in the supreme authority of medieval Christendom was derived from a religious conception of authority, which veiled the coercive element in the structure. It was the possession of the 'keys of heaven' by the Pope that could hold people in thrall by the sanction of excommunication, and kings in awe by the sanction of interdiction, which was the threat of removing the divine sanction of royal authority." One of the reasons why the peculiar partnership between the church and empire arose was, as Niebuhr points out, the need of the church to have its Charlemagne, that is, a "police arm of the church, since the church, as a spiritual kingdom, could not use force."[28]

Such arrangements are unnecessary for the modern church, since it does not have the kind of general political responsibility borne by the medieval church. But within its own political perimeter the church today may be equally inhibited in the "use of force," that is, in the outward exhibition of aggressive power within its organization. And thus, in the internal politics of the church, a great deal of ingenuity may have to be exercised in terms of rationalization and institutional camouflage to "veil" the coercive element in the structure, and, in general, to pretend that the power factor is not significant in the operations.

At times in its history, and in some Christian circles today, the church is held up as the model and prototype of the ideal state. But it may well be that, politically speaking, the secular state is the model and prototype of the church, especially insofar as secular politics in a democratic state may be a healthier demonstration of the rational and creative harnessing of man's aggressive instincts, that is, his powers, and more honestly realized than the religious community has been able to achieve in its politics. As Anthony Storrs puts it: "As a practical system for controlling and making use of the competitive aggression which is so evident in political controversy, democracy seems the best system yet devised. Although slow and uncertain in operation, democracy has the decided advantage over other political systems of providing an opposition which not only acts as a check on government, but also gives scope for passionate disagreement. Indeed, the House of Commons might stand as an exemplar of how men should deal with their aggressive drives: for it provides 'enemies' who are clearly serving a useful function; it encourages the expression of opposite opinion; yet by bringing opponents face to face as human beings, it makes it difficult for them to project paranoid images upon each other. . . . it is hard to fault democracy as an ideal psychologically."[29]

The creative transformation of power for constructive purposes and goals is a major test of church politics, just as it is the challenge for all other political life.

The church may find some consolation in the fact that it is not alone in its frustrations in trying to find an adequate politics for the structuring and controlling of the power elements in its communal existence. Erich Fromm has pointed out "the peculiar quasi-political character of the psychoanalytic movement." The congresses "had all the earmarks of a political convention," the leaders were engaged in politically "attacking and appeasing, rather than the attitude of scientists concerned with the discussion of their subject matter," sects arose which were "the same as in other aggressive religious and political movements centered around a dogma and the idolization of the leader," and the whole development was politicized by Freud, who, "under the disguise of a scientific school" actually talked "the language of an empire builder or political leader.

The boy who admired Marshal Massena, the adolescent who wanted to be a liberal or socialist political leader, the grown-up man, who identified himself with Hannibal and Moses, saw in his creation, the psychoanalytic movement, the instrument to save—and to conquer—the world for an ideal."[30]

One may look upon this as another piece of evidence, if it be needed, that man is a political animal. No amount of religious piety or psychological sophistication is able to comprehend the limits of his imagination or plumb the depths of his creativity. His political activity, in whatever form, is the intricate interweaving of all these disparate elements of his nature and environment. And if the rational and intuitive, the artistic and scientific, control of power in politics often seems beyond man's capacities, that is not so much an indication of man's weakness and limitations but a sign of man's noble aspiration to search out the ultimate meaning of life, and to realize as fully as possible his created powers.

4-*Participation*

You Can't Take People Out of
Participation, But . . .

Impasse in Texas Catholic Revolt

SAN ANTONIO, TEX. "We're headed for a more democratic
church, one that belongs to the people."

The speaker was Joe Bernal, a dapper 42-year-old Mexican-
American state senator who is part of a grass-roots revolt that
is seeking to bring about radical changes in the style of government of the Roman Catholic archbishop of San Antonio.

The revolt began nearly two years ago among local priests
who sought more freedom for themselves and a more radical
stance by their church on social issues. It has now spread to
middle-class laymen with similar concerns.

Role

Inspired by the pronouncements of the ecumenical council
of 1962 to 1965, both groups see a greater role for laymen and
priests in the government of their church.

Both are also becoming increasingly impatient with what
they regard as a contradiction between the authoritarian ecclesiastical traditions of their church and the current secular
movements for human rights.

As a result, the half-million-member archdiocese of San
Antonio has become in recent weeks a virtual microcosm of the
divisive struggles taking place throughout the Catholic church as

it seeks to adjust its policies to the demands of present day society.

The revolt took on major proportions on October 24, when 31 local priests released a letter they had sent to Pope Paul VI and other high Catholic officials demanding the removal of their 77-year-old archbishop, the Most Rev. Robert E. Lucey.

Six days later Archbishop Lucey reacted by suspending four signers of the letter from their posts at Assumption Seminary on the ground that the imprudence of their "recent public actions" had made them unfit for office.

The dismissed officials, who included the seminary rector, the Rev. Roy Rihn, have rented a house in a low-income area and are taking secular jobs.

Protest

The dismissals drew loud protests from a variety of groups within the archdiocese, including most of the 160 seminarians, the officially sponsored senate of priests, an unofficial priests' association and the six-month-old association for lay involvement.

The latter, a group of 100 laymen, most of them from prosperous north side parishes, has collected the signatures of more than 7,000 people on a petition urging the archbishop's retirement.

Last week both a "neutral observer" appointed by the apostolic delegate, or papal representative, in Washington and an 18-member fact-finding board appointed by Archbishop Lucey held hearings and tried to sift through a maze of charges, countercharges and conflicting statements of fact.

Task

It was not an easy task, however, and few persons see an early end to the conflict.

"There's such an impasse that nothing the archbishop says registers with the laymen and priests, and nothing they say registers with him," said the Rev. William C. Martin, the Irish-born chairman of the fact-finding group. "We have a complete breakdown of trust on both sides."

The archbishop is a shy, Los Angeles-born administrator who is a friend of President Johnson and a supporter of the war in Vietnam. He has ruled the archdiocese of San Antonio since

1941 and earned a reputation as a staunch liberal on social issues.

Style

Despite his liberalism, however, his style of operation has been highly authoritarian and based on the theological premise that his own word as archbishop was the word of the church.

Such methods began to produce conflict in February, 1967, when the Rev. Sherrill Smith and the Rev. William Killian, two priests of the archdiocese, were sent on a five-day disciplinary retreat for taking part in a farm workers' strike in a neighboring diocese against the archbishop's orders to stay away.

This was followed by a series of what appeared to be punitive transfers of priests who had challenged the archbishop in one way or another.

Visit

Almost all of a group of 10 priests who visited Archbishop Lucey to protest the action against the two strike supporters, for instance, were subsequently moved to new posts.

In some cases the facts surrounding the transfers are clouded. Supporters of the archbishop argue, for instance, that the four suspended seminary officials would have been transferred anyway because of their educational policies.

Under the ousted regime the institution earned a reputation of one of the best diocesan seminaries in the country, but its progressive policies drew fire from some quarters.

The constant repetition of questionable incidents, however, has produced widespread resentment among both laymen and priests.

Methods

Others defend Archbishop Lucey's methods and argue that far from being outdated, they are necessary for the continued health of the church.

Some of the dissident priests believe that they made a tactical error in demanding his removal, since any such action by the Vatican in the near future would seem like caving in to pressure from the priests and laymen.

Others, however, take the position that Rome needed to be shown that his removal was essential.

"There will just be a slowdown in all aspects of church life until he goes," one priest said. "Priests will do less in their parishes, and laymen won't get involved."

New York Times[1]

A Priests' Rebellion In Germany

BONN, WEST GERMANY Rebellious young Catholic priests in West Germany are demanding a say in the election of their bishops and an end to celibacy.

Clerical discontent is also being fanned by the controversial birth-control issue and the Vatican's reemphasis of its ecclesiastical authority.

Unconfirmed reports said an increasing number of discouraged priests left their parishes this year, but official church authorities describe the reports as exaggerated.

However, several priests, some of whom recently renounced the priesthood, are openly grumbling about what they call the "autocratic medieval attitude" of the church.

Psychologist

A former priest in the Westphalian city of Paderborn, now a married man, said he felt deeply humiliated at having to answer some 100 questions on his private life when he asked to be relieved of his vows.

A psychologist alleged that quite a large proportion of the country's 20,000 priests are having trouble over their vow of celibacy. Groups of young priests plan to confront their bishops with a critical resolution on the problem early next year.

In Siegen, North Rhine Westphalia, theologian Johannes Hoffman wants to set up an organization to mediate between the church and dissident priests.

He said in a newspaper interview that several of his friends would have liked to continue as priests—as long as they could marry too.

A leftwing movement also is gaining ground among young priests and Catholic laymen influenced by the nonconformism of the country's radical students.

This year this movement surfaced as the "Solidarity Group of Catholic Priests" in Bochum, in the industrial Ruhr.

In Freiburg, Cologne and Speyer, other restless priests demanded a say in the election of bishops.

Attitude

Symptomatic of the wave of unrest was the headline-catching case this month of an abbot who asked the Vatican to relieve him of his post because he objected to "the church's authoritarian attitude."

Abbot Dr. Alkuin Heising, 41, from the 900-year old Benedictine monastery at Siegburg, near Bonn, said the church was suppressing all attempts to reform it and pursuing "a selfish aim" in its relationship with modern society.

Disobedience among Catholic laymen reached a peak at a five-day Catholic congress in Dortmund in September. The young people challenged the Pope's encyclical on birth control.

One poster held up during one of the many discussions simply read "Don't talk about the pill. We take it."

Reuters[2]

World Council of Churches at Uppsala

. . .

The fact is that considerable strength and ingenuity is required to make any kind of impact on a gathering of over 2,000 people. Individuals and small groups are completely dwarfed by the scale of the setting and nothing more modest than a brass band could be certain of a hearing.

Eclipse of Democracy

This raises a number of crucial points about the organisation of an Assembly of this kind and I hope that someone has been making a careful study of the eclipse of democracy in the Uppsala gathering. When a distinguished judge of the Supreme Court in West Germany produced a resolution asking for the removal from the hall of plainclothed policemen this fell to the ground for the apparent lack of a seconder. In point of fact, Geoffrey Ainger, who is not exactly a midget, was on his feet and waving his arm aloft to support the judge, but he could not be seen by the chairman on the distant rostrum.

Then there was the occasion of the election of members of the Faith and Order committee. A number of substitute names were produced by way of amendment to the list provided by the nominations committee which was fair enough, but there were no speeches to indicate why a particular replacement was considered necessary. So the delegates voted quite blindly and an excellent man like William Stringfellow was removed from the committee as a result of a plot led by the Presiding Bishop of the Protestant Episcopal Church of the USA: hardly any of those who voted him off were aware that he had committed the unpardonable crime of being rude about the Presiding Bishop in his book on the Bishop Pike affair.

On the other hand, a movement from the floor to secure the appointment of a laywoman as one of the six presidents of the WCC almost succeeded. There were only 50 votes between the virtually unknown Mrs. Birgit Rodhe of Sweden and the famous Bishop Hans Lilje of Germany—the first occasion on which an official nomination has been challenged. This narrow squeeze undoubtedly prepared the way for Pauline Webb's election as one of the two vice-chairmen of the Central Committee.

Youthful Voices

In the circumstances, the youth participants did a remarkably useful job. Without voting power and lacking the political know how and experience to influence a large-scale international meeting, they nonetheless made their voices heard and kept the delegates on their toes. No doubt they were on occasion irresponsible—who wasn't?—but there was never a chance that anyone would be allowed to get away with a statement which was not related to the needs of the under-privileged. Offence was naturally caused by the publication of a poster asking why the "German church bosses" were travelling about Uppsala in their chauffeur-driven Mercedes: Did they not care for the smell of the other delegates in the buses? Or were they too old and weak? Or were they just showing off? They had, suggested the poster, come *per Mercedes Episcoporum* instead of *per pedes apostolorum.*

All very trivial, no doubt, but it seems no bad thing that the young people should regard the church as a community in which straight questions can be asked. And it is surely valuable that the documents of a solemn Assembly should be subjected to the same analysis and scathing comment that would be accorded to incompetence in, say, politics: "some paragraphs are so 'perfect' and insignificant that they could be found in any dogmatics." WCC delegates and statesmen are not of course used to this. It is good that their initiation has at last begun.

More positive, as the elderly are wont to say, was the impressive fast on behalf of the hungry world which the young people organised in the final week of the Assembly, and also their cross-examination of leading delegates at "Club 68" every evening at 10:30. How else might we have known that the Archbishop of Canterbury is in favour of inter-communion once serious negotiations have started between separated churches.[3]

It is a commonplace among anthropologists that most, if not all, of the major institutions of civilized society have their origins in primitive life and that though new external forms have developed in the process of transmission through the generations, yet at their center the primitive core remains. Among primitive people political rule is intimately connected with magic. Bertrand de Jouvenel writes: "Among primitive peoples the royal road to political rule is an understanding of the will of the occult powers and a knowledge of the times in which and the conditions under which they will be favourable. The Elders are the natural repository of this branch of knowledge. . . . The inner circle is formed by those of the Elders who are most deeply versed in the occult sciences, and to them the whole tribe is subject."[4]

As has been suggested, the element of magic is always present—sometimes overt, sometimes hidden—in religious institutions. Religious leaders, therefore, have access to political power not only through ordinary political channels but also through the occult and magical powers which are ascribed to them. The consent of the governed required for effective political rule may be obtained by a priest-politician not only through secular political means, whatever these may be, but also by the magical aura which surrounds him as a religious figure. In other words, his priestly mystique is part—in some cases even the predominant part—of his *political* effectiveness.

Secular politics provides for correction of political leaders—largely through regular elections in which old leaders may be repudiated and new leaders chosen to take their place. In church politics, however, this may be much more difficult, not because the constitutional means are not available for this kind of redress on the part of a constituency but because, whatever formal means are open for correcting or changing leadership, there may be deep psychological inhibitions against touching the "taboo" object—the priest-magician—by the devotees. The church politician, therefore, has often been immune from the public kind of corrective and disciplinary forces which are so acutely felt by the secular politician. The secular politician may be voted out of office simply on the whimsical popular assumption that "it is time to throw the rascals out." In the ethos of the church, however, it is hard for the constituency to separate their natural distrust of politicians from their religious respect for religious leaders. Political housecleaning, then, becomes more complicated in church than in secular politics. Healthy politics requires a strong dose of skepticism on the part of those governed; they learn to trust their leaders only to the extent that such trust is required for the political process to carry on. In a religious association, on the other hand, the members have traditionally been encouraged to trust leaders as divinely ordained; therefore, public skepticism about motives as well as policies and programs is not as strong an influence on ecclessiastical as on those in other political institutions.

One of the fundamental reasons for the separation of ceremonial and legislative authority in the British political system—vested in the monarch and the prime minister, respectively—is the recognition of the residual magical aura surrounding a hereditary sovereign, of the "divinity which doth hedge a king." As Walter Bagehot observes in *The English Constitution,* such a primitive superstitious attitude "may have less sanctity than it had, but it still has much sanctity. . . . The best instance is Lord Chatham, the most dictatorial and imperious of English statesmen, and almost the first English statesman who was borne into power against the wishes of the king and against the wishes of the nobility—the first popular minister. We might have expected a proud tribune of the people to be dictatorial to his sovereign—to be to the king what he was to all others. On the contrary, he was slave of his own imagination; there was a kind of mystic enchantment in the vicinity of the monarch which divested him of his ordinary nature. 'The least peek into the king's closet', said Mr. Burke, 'intoxicates him, and will to the end of his life.' A wit said that, even at the levee, he bowed so low that you could see the tip of his hooked nose between his legs. He was in the habit of kneeling at the bedside of George III while transacting business. Now no man can *argue* on his knees. The same superstitious feeling which keeps him in that physical attitude will keep him in a corresponding mental attitude."[5]

It is obvious that the same dynamics are operative in respect to church politics, with the additional factor that the religious element heightens the superstitious feelings and the sense of "mystic enchantment" in the presence of the church sovereign. The image that immediately springs to mind in this connection is, of course, the baroque pageantry surrounding the public appearances of the pope. Pope John in particular sought to limit these displays, which he, and many others, felt were more appropriate to the court of a Byzantine despot than to the house of a servant of the people of God and a leader of an increasingly democratized church.

However, many Protestant ministers in ordinary congregations are touched by the same forces of magical deification. The general trend is away from authoritarian and paternalistic forms of ministerial leadership. Nevertheless, as with the pope *par excellence,* so the Protestant minister not infrequently finds that his priestly and political roles become mixed and confused in the minds of the members of the congregation. The minister is in two senses an administrator: on one hand, he is ordained to administer the sacraments and, on the other, he is the "prime minister" of the congregation as an organizational entity. But the authoritative mystique which surrounds his sacerdotal functions inevitably intrudes on his political functions. And so, in varying degrees depending on his own abilities and on the context in which he is working, the minister as politician is bolstered in his power by his position as priest, the dispenser of the "mysteries." This kind of political sacerdotalism is most clearly evidenced in those polities which require that the priest shall, by definition, be the head of the church council, or equivalent congregational governing entity.

It is generally conceded that one of the major causes for the "maceration" (Joseph Sittler) of the clergy at this time, as well as one of the prime reasons for disaffection with the parish ministry, is the crisis in regard to ministerial authority and the general lack of consensus on the proper role of the minister and the extent and limits of his powers. In a sense, one could call this a political crisis for the ministry. On one hand, the authority of the minister is relatively unchallenged in the sacramental sphere: that is, he can expect that his formal role as chief administrator of the liturgical and sacramental activities of the congregation will be generally accepted. On the other hand, his political role is not nearly as well defined. Here his authority depends very much on his own personal talents and upon the character and attitude of the congregation he serves.

As has been suggested, the old pattern in which the authority exercised in the "spiritual" realm could be transferred to the political areas of the congregation's life is increasingly questioned. It can no longer be taken for granted. For instance, unlike in past days, the pastor-priest must be very politically sensitive as to how far he may exhibit the style of "father" (in God)—which is expected and accepted in the sacramental and liturgical roles he performs—in the political affairs of the church. In the latter, such a style is likely to be termed "paternalistic" and will be resented and resisted. Furthermore, in the egalitarian and democratic ethos of the modern world, the minister may himself have an uneasy conscience about paternal-

istic authority which he politically wields. This may exist only
at an unconscious level, just as the resentment of the congregation against such forms of political domination may also
be subconscious. The point is, however, that whether it is a
Roman Catholic bishop or a Protestant parish minister, church
leaders are operating without any commonly agreed political standards or any generally agreed political principles for
exercising authority. The minister or priest in his liturgical
garb standing at an altar or in the pulpit is a symbol of authority. The same person sitting at a congregational council meeting in a business suit is increasingly looked upon as one—perhaps first—among equals.

This may be deplored or welcomed. The fact is, however,
that the community's well-being depends upon both the sacramental and the political functions being adequately met.
In most cases, the ordained minister is responsible for both.
In this sense, it could be said that the modern minister wields
two swords, spiritual and secular, in the congregation. The
danger is that he may be tempted to draw upon his sacramental
authority to buttress his position as political manager of the
congregation, or even to camouflage his political ineptitude.
Or, from the other side, the laity may be so antagonistic to
clerical control, and so much in reaction against the older forms
of political paternalism in the church, that they refuse to allow
the governmental freedom and discretion to their ordained
pastor without which he is unable to function politically in
any creative or responsible way.

The dilemma that is being posed is essentially political.
The problem is that the church generally has denied its character as a political institution, has camouflaged its political
processes, and has refused to admit the political responsibilities of its leaders. More and more, however, the church constituency is becoming politically sensitized and in respect to
church leaders is using secular models, particularly those derived from participatory democracy and political activism, to
assess them and judge their performance. Church politicians operating in a democratic political environment, for example, are

going to be measured by the operative political assumptions of that society. The autocratic and monarchical bishop or pastor, for example, may be accepted as authority in spite of his anachronistic political style, but only so long as there is still enough magical mystique about the church and its leadership to allow this kind of incongruity. Eventually, however, such political anachronism is its own downfall because the conscious and subconscious political responses and instincts of the governed are more and more divorced from purely authoritarian, top-down, political models. Under such circumstances, genuine political consent soon degenerates into formal lip-service, or, on the other hand, into subversive or overt revolutionary action and confrontation.

This whole process of political degeneration is only accelerated, of course, when the ecclesiastical authorities become ideologically inflexible or revert to authoritarian repression as a defensive political device. For example, Pericle Cardinal Felici in an editorial in the Vatican's newspaper *L'Osservatore Romano* compares present-day Roman Catholic dissenters to heretics of earlier times and argues: "To want to introduce democracy in the church, as if it were a worldly society, means to go against the very plan of Christ. . . means to open the door to disorders and insubordinations without end." It is evident here that the constitutional hierarchical structure of the church is considered identical with a certain monarchical and oligarchical political pattern of ecclesiastical authority. Cardinal Felici exhibits an institutional and political fundamentalism which identifies form with content. It is historically and sociologically understandable why the monarchical political form is for some so closely identified psychologically with papal (and ecclesiastical) authority. But this is no dogmatic reason for asserting such authority to be exercised responsibly. Indeed, on the contrary, it may be argued that the only way for ecclesiastical authority to be exercised responsibly today is for that authority to be expressed in democratic models and procedures.

It may well be, for example, that only a democratically

elected hierarchy has any possibility of exercising authority in a real way politically. And it may well be that a popularly elected pope, bishop, priest (or Protestant church president or local pastor) is the only political mode through which religious leadership can effectively operate on the modern scene. This is, of course, no argument for absolutizing democracy as the only conceivable political form for church life. Ideologically, however, democracy tends to be the *modus vivendi* for modern man's political aspirations and activities. Even though (as Bertrand Russell and other political philosophers have pointed out) the virtues of democracy may be largely negative, there seems to be consonance between the fundamental Christian dogmatic principle of men's equality in Christ and the democratic political principle of universal franchise.

Be that as it may, if democracy is accepted as the most viable political system for realizing a free and humane society, can political democracy be expressed in the church? Can church politics be democratic? One must admit that to define democracy itself is no easy task. In general, one might define it as that political system through which the greatest degree of participation on the part of the citizenry is provided for, facilitated, and guaranteed. As Harold Laski once put it: "For democracy, with all its weaknesses, enables the widest body of demand to be taken into account in shaping the legal imperatives of a state. It makes criticism of their operation the basis of their life. It increases initiative by widening the sense of responsibility. It gives the citizen not merely the sense of sharing in decision, but the actual opportunity to influence its substance. Granted, as experience seems to suggest, that a democratic system is bound to work more slowly than its alternative, simply because the variety of wills it encounters is so much greater, there is no other system which has the same merit of meeting, as an institutional scheme, the theoretical end that the state must serve.

"But to say that a state requires democratic form is not to settle the institutions through which that form receives expression; for broadly speaking, it is not untrue to say that democracy has not, in any certain fashion, discovered its appropriate institutions."[6]

In this context, and with these qualifications, it could be argued that if the new ecclesiological trend in Christian theology is toward more social and dynamic concepts—for example, "the People of God" as the decisive ecclesiological image in the Constitution on the Church of Vatican II—a more democratic form of church politics might be the appropriate institutional response of the church in its organizational life to this theological accent. To acknowledge, paraphrasing Laski, that church democracy has not, in any certain fashion, discovered its appropriate institutions, nevertheless, is far from admitting that democracy in the church is "against the very plan of Christ." Church democracy may take on special forms and institutional characteristics appropriate to its fundamental nature and purposes, but this adaptation would not necessarily negate the basic democratic principle.

As has been said, the crucial test of any democratic politics is the extent to which it allows, facilitates, and guarantees universal participation. In a democracy, this is most meaningfully expressed through elections. The power of the ballot and universal voting privilege is the heart of the democratic system. Lest this be thought irrelevant to the life of the church, it is interesting to note that democratic procedures are already evident in the early history of the church. The book of Acts, for example, reflects the idea (the actual practice would be more difficult to determine) that church officials are to be chosen by the members. The successor to Judas among the Twelve was chosen by lots, but two nominees were selected by the group beforehand. And the Seven—the forerunners of the diaconate theoretically—were selected by the group and then confirmed by the Twelve. In other words, there emerges, however shadowy, the picture of a democratic political process in the primitive church for selecting leadership and for filling positions of authority.

Though it is difficult to determine whether the account in Acts represents general practice in the primitive church, it seems evident from later developments that the process described in Acts 6:1ff., namely, ordination to ecclesiastical office on the basis of popular election ("pick out from among you seven men . . . whom we may appoint to this duty"), is not considered strange in many parts of the Christian community. Cyprian, for example, assumes that part of the "liturgy" of the laity is that of "electing" and a corollary of his "high view of the clergyman as the steward of God was that the people of God had the power of choosing their bishops, presbyters, and deacons and rejecting the unworthy."[7] In fact, it was not until the eleventh century in the West that the idea of lay participation in church politics was given a major set-back with the foundation of the College of Cardinals "established with the function of choosing popes quite independently of any lay directives."[8] The "laymen" in this case were the kings and emperors, and so church "democracy" is hardly the point at issue but, rather, the canonical question of the right of laity to elect.

In other words, the general tradition in church government through the ages has been that of popular participation in church politics. And though this tradition may have been obscured and lost sight of in later periods, the Christian community in the earlier ages never considered the idea of popular political processes of election intrinsically incompatible with the idea that those ecclesiastical officials so chosen were divinely instituted authorities. One rather strange testimony to the strength of this political tradition is the elevation of celibacy to canon-law requirement for clergy through the Gregorian reforms. One of the specific reasons for doing so was the fear of hereditary bishoprics and the desire to break up entrenched familial political monopolies in church life. The result, as even so severe a critic as Bertrand Russell admits, was an institution in which, unlike most of its secular counterparts, a person had the possibility of rising to positions of eminence and power with little else to achieve these laurels than personal talent and individual merit. Furthermore, the College of Cardinals itself, entrusted with the responsibility of electing the pope, whatever its limitations as a political instrumentality viewed from modern perspectives, can be seen both as the vestigial remains as well as the potential promise of representative and democratic church government. For, as secular political history shows, democratic development can take place within the older governmental forms, thus providing for continuity and innovation—both necessary for vital political life.

The Code of Canon Law illustrates this double-sided approach to church politics. Canon 171, which deals with the authority of the Roman Pontiff, asserts that the pope, as successor to the primacy of St. Peter, has the supreme and full power of jurisdiction over the universal church, not only in matters of faith and morals but also in those pertaining to the discipline and government of the Roman Church throughout the world. The Code also affirms that this power is independent of all human authority. However, this "full power of supreme jurisdiction by divine right" is only realized through a legitimate election (Canons 123-141) and only becomes effective and is obtained at the moment the pope-elect accepts the election.

The novel of Morris West, *Shoes of the Fisherman,* has brilliantly dramatized this electoral procedure in the College of Cardinals. Cloaked as it is in the antique customs of a bygone day, the ceremonial of the pope's election is nevertheless a fact of great political significance. *De facto* the pope is an elective official. It may be said, as one commentary on the Code of Canon Law puts it, that the "position of the Roman Pontiff is altogether without parallel in the world. In all other independent human organizations and societies, the form of government is dependent on the will of the majority, but the form of government of the Church is fixed by Christ, and thus cannot be changed by men. The authority of the Supreme Pontiff does not come from the Church, but from Christ. All that the Church can do is to determine the manner of electing her Supreme Head. The power of the Pope comes directly from God, for he is not merely the representative of the people of the Church, but the representative of Christ."[9]

The implied contradiction between the authority of the pope (derived from Christ) and his election (determined by the church), and the absolute distinction made between the form of government of the church (fixed by Christ) and the form of government of other independent human organizations and societies (dependent on the will of the majority) are vestigial remnants of magical thinking about political leadership in the Code of Canon Law. When the commentator argues that "All that the Church can do is to determine the manner of electing her Supreme Head," legally speaking he is perfectly correct. Politically speaking, however, this freedom and right of election means much more than the strict technicalities of the law suggest. The determination of the "manner of electing," which is the province of human responsibility in the Roman Church in regard to the pope, also—potentially at least— determines the "manner" of the one who is elected. And the political leader's "manner" determines how the divine "form of government . . . fixed by Christ" is related to the "will of the majority." The one who is elected determines, by his own personal, dogmatic, psychological, and canonical self-image, how and in what way his God-given power is related to his position as both the "representative of the people of the Church" and "the representative of Christ." As in other political institutions, the office shapes the person but the person also shapes the office. Even in modern times, the varieties of men with their contrasting "manners" who have put on the shoes of the fisherman indicates how differently the Petrine office can be interpreted by successive popes and how sharply divergent political styles and administrative methods may be even when legally restricted by the strict technicalities of the Code of Canon Law as well as by popular stereotypes of papal form.

The Texas Catholic Revolt is, as the *New York Times* says, "a virtual microcosm of the divisive struggles taking place through the Catholic church as it seeks to adjust its policies to the demands of present day society." As such it also illustrates the importance of a clear dogmatic distinction between the authority assigned to particular ecclesiastical offices and the historically conditioned, and thus relative, power exercised by the person holding such an office. The Texas Revolt is clearly directed against the person and not the office, and thus it becomes primarily a political rather than a constitutional issue. The protesting priests and laymen are not, as far as can be determined, seeking to undermine or to abolish the office of archbishop. They are, however, seeking to unseat the office-holder. Basically, it is a familiar political phenomenon. Within the church, however, it becomes a traumatic crisis. Part of the reason for this political escalation is the generation gap between an elderly feudalistic leader with an authoritarian political style and a younger group of priests and laymen committed to the ideal of a "more democratic church, one that belongs to the people." But this ideological gap is accentuated because the archdiocese has no political structures adequate to moderate this conflict or political means to reconcile the contradictory assumptions and expectations of the parties involved. This, like most violent revolutions, represents a breakdown of traditional political institutions, a mutual loss of trust between conflicting power groups, and is a sign of fundamental political bankruptcy of a community. Or, to put it another way, the politics of a top-down authority structure comes into direct conflict with the politics of a grass-roots democratic movement and, unless a new politics can be devised which incorporates both groups within a common political process, anarchy and revolution is almost inevitable. The only form of political communication becomes "non-negotiable" confrontation. Whatever canonical authority an archbishop, or any other church leader official, possesses, and however firm his constitutional position may be, the actual power he is able to wield depends not on his formal status but on his political possibilities. A secular political corollary may be seen in the admission of former President Lyndon B. Johnson that in retrospect he finds the major failing of his administration not in the policies pursued (which he still supports as right) but that young people, in particular, lost confidence in their government because the politicians had not "opened the process of decision-making . . . more fully to the public." Thus, Mr. Johnson said, there arose "feelings that democratic channels were not adequate for the expression of . . . disagreement." It is his conclusion that however meritorious or justifiable programs and policies may be, they are "meaningless unless young people feel a basic trust and understanding of the process of their government."[10]

One might well argue, therefore, that the dogmatic mystiques about the power and authority of an ecclesiastical leader are becoming somewhat irrelevant to the actual political power and authority which such a leader wields. Insofar as magical concepts of leadership still have some force in the religious circle, these dogmatic mystiques bear some actual political weight. If, for example, the ordinary member of a religious organization believes that the leader's power and authority "comes directly from God" and that this power and authority are unqualified, his response to it is bound to be passive and subservient. If, however, he begins to realize that he has some political responsibility for determining *who* shall bear this kind of power and responsibility, a new political dimension has opened up in his relation to the ecclesiastical leadership. In this way, rational concepts of political process gradually force out more primitive magical superstitions and dogmatic mystiques.

Reinhold Niebuhr argues that "free societies are the fortunate products of the confluence of Christian and secular forces." For example, both Calvinism and secular rationalism contributed "to the challenge of religiously sanctified political authority," both in Europe and in America. Or, to put it another way, "secularism is an aid in delivering traditional societies from their idolatries" because it has helped "to make genuinely secular (that is, non-sacred) objects and ends of human striving morally respectable." To some extent one could argue that voting in an election is both a sacred and a non-sacred symbol in politics. On one hand, it represents the pragmatic necessity of struggling and competing for power in order for political responsibility to be assigned and assumed. On the other hand, it represents the religious conviction that each individual has inalienable rights and unique worth and dignity by nature. Niebuhr continues: "Democracy as a political institution is rooted in the principle of universal suffrage; which arms every citizen with political power and the chance to veto the actions of his rulers. It implements the thesis that governments derive their authority from the consent of the governed. Both clerical absolutism and orthodox Protestantism's principle of the divine right of kings had to be challenged before political democracy could arise."[11]

The point here is simply that once the fact of election is introduced into ecclesiological theory, the political implications are incalculable. For however exalted the position which the dogma assigns the pope and however unlimited his power and authority are from that dogmatic perspective, in political reality his position is dependent on ordinary political factors and his power and authority qualified by innumerable non-sacred influences. According to Jerome Frank, in his iconoclastic book on legal theory *Law and the Modern Mind,* there is "a strong tendency to convert fictions and hypotheses into dogmas." This is because, he says (following Vaihinger), "to entertain ideas of less fixed character than dogmas involves a condition of tension extremely disagreeable to the mind which tries to bring ideas into equilibrium and to establish an unbroken connection between them."[12]

A vivid illustration of this discrepancy between the theoretical dogmatic authority of the pope and his actual political power is found in the story related about Pope John before the convocation of Vatican II: "At this juncture the pope spoke to four or five of the oldest cardinals, asking them to relinquish their positions as heads of Congregations. After the interview, the pope was seen standing in some amazement, shaking his head and saying out loud: 'But they refused, they refused! Never in my life did I think anyone would refuse the pope.'"[13]

In a political sense, then, one could say that the absolute authority and power of the pope is a legal fiction, which, in

Judge Frank's words, has been "converted into dogma." The same could be said of the "fiction" of infallibility; in this case, it is being argued by some Catholic canonists, the terms for infallability set by the Vatican Council I in 1870 are incapable of being met, at least in the present state of division in the Roman Church. Be that as it may, the simple political fact that the pope is elected means that all the theoretical dogmatic assumptions about his power and authority are absolutely qualified. It means, in the words of Karl Rahner, the Austrian Jesuit, that the "office and sovereign power" of the pope are not (as in the case of a hereditary monarchy, for example) "independent of the intellectual and moral decisions of men." In this sense, though the Pope canonically possesses *supreme et plena potestas jurisdictiionis vere episcopalis, orinaria et immediata,* he is not, according to Rahner, "absolute monarch" of the Roman Church, for here "the bearer of supreme power is ever and again .designated by election, i.e., by a free, deliberate act of men themselves. This also holds true where the actual content of power subsists independent of the electors. Even here the *exercise* of this power is deeply influenced by the historical, the elective character of the chosen ruler, and therefore by the character of his electors as well. To define the Church as a monarchy is to fail to throw into relief the scope which, as history shows, here remains for the play of the charismatic and unexpected qualities of the Church's character, her perennial youthfulness, her vigour."[14]

Furthermore, as Hans Küng points out in *Structures of the Church,* the Roman Church has canonical redress against a mentally ill, or schismatic, or heretical pope. Thus, as in the case of mental illness (because, as Küng puts it, "a man does not become pope on the basis of hereditary succession but on the basis of his personal qualities"), there may arise "extraordinary situations in Church history when a pope not only may resign but also must resign." Küng believes this principle should be followed even in the case of a loss of popular confidence in a pope: "If a pope sees that his person—guilty or not—is no longer able to fulfill this fundamental function of the Petrine office, he is morally obliged to give up his office for the sake of the unity and peace of the Church, as well as for the sake of a more credible presentation of the Petrine office, and voluntarily make way for another pope who can more properly perform this fundamental function of the Petrine office."[15]

But *who* is to exert the pressure for this political decision? *Who* is to exercise the political power? *Who* is to cast the ballot? According to present practice, the pope is elected by the College of Cardinals. They, in the words of one canonist, "constitute the Senate of the Roman Pontiff" and assist him in the government of the Roman Church as "principal advisers and assistants." At the same time, they might also be considered (according to Rahner) "a kind of committee or executive of the episcopal college, to which the election of the pope most appropriately belongs as a result of the ultimate constitutional structure of the Church."[16]

This, of course, is precisely the point at issue in the current debates regarding "democracy" in the church. For it is not only a question of laymen (and ordinary priests) sharing in the shaping of ecclesiastical policy, but also the possibilities of their participating in ecclesiastical elections, and—as in the Case of the Texas Catholic Revolt—initiating deposition proceedings against ecclesiastical officials. This demand for "a more democratic church, one that belongs to the people," obviously threatens any ecclesiastical power elite, especially if this power rests on oligarchical or tyrannical foundations.

The first line of defense is to stifle criticism. As Pedro Arrupe, S.J., told *Ya,* the Madrid Catholic daily newspaper, soon after being elected superior general of the Society of Jesus: "I am strictly opposed to criticism of the church. If reforms should be made, this will be done by the duly constituted hierarchy. . . . It is intolerable that any defect of the church, however real, should be broached publicly by individuals or groups, regardless of the good will they might have. If the person who is critical is intelligent, he will be understanding and see that the best solution will be either to keep silent and wait . . . or meekly bring the defects to the knowledge of the proper authority. Cheap coffeehouse criticism accomplishes nothing. The church will provide in the manner and at the time it deems proper. One should never undertake criticism of one's own. The only thing that can result from criticizing is the creation of the climate of confusion, and the obstruction, if not paralysis, of the work of the church in behalf of all."

Whatever the merit of this viewpoint, it is obviously one which only an aristocratic authority beyond the political control of the public could afford. It is also an attitude which increases the alienation of the constituency from the leadership of the churches. For ordinary members today, as well as local priests, are increasingly influenced by democratic political notions and attitudes. They are better informed, and therefore more critical, of both leaders and their policies over which they feel they have little control, than the previous generation among whom such populist views were almost unknown, indeed almost unthinkable.

The second line of defense by ecclesiastical authorities against pressure for wider political participation in church affairs has been the line of tradition. The argument here is that lay participation in church politics is novel, and therefore suspect, if not illicit. Vatican II struck one blow against this reading of tradition. Ecclesiologically, the Council stressed the idea of church as "the new People of God" and also emphasized the "interrelated" character of the common priesthood of the laity and the ministerial or hierarchical priesthood: "Each of them in its own special way is a participation in the one priesthood of Christ." Vatican II still maintains the traditional position that the *government* of the church rests in the hands of the hierarchy—the College of Bishops with the pope. Nevertheless, there is evident in various of the Vatican II documents a significant shift in emphasis even at this point. For example, in the *Decree on the Ministry and Life of Priests* it is suggested that the bishop should have discussions with the priests "about those matters which concern the necessities of pastoral work and the welfare of the diocese." The *Decree* goes on to affirm that: "In order to put these ideals into effect, a group or senate of priests representing the presbytery should be established. It is to operate in a manner adapted to modern circumstances and needs and have a form and norms to be determined by law. By its counsel, this body will be able to give effective assistance to the bishop in his government of the diocese."[17] Canon lawyers have pointed out, however, that this diocesan "Presbyterium" is not intended to be a parallel to the College of Bishops. The latter is "an institution of divine law; the diocesan 'Presbyterium' is an institution of ecclesiastical law." It is clear, nonetheless, that this broadening of the collegial principle in church government marks a definitely democratic trend in Roman Catholic ecclesiastical politics.

Also, it is clear that if such a presbyterial arrangement is "to operate in a manner adapted to modern circumstances" it inevitably means increasing involvement of the laity in church government, even if in the first instance this is only through the mediation of the priests in their "Presbyterium." Here again, however, the legal fiction of the Code of Canon Law that only the hierarchy governs the church is shattered by the real participation of priests and laity in the political dynamics of church life. Protests themselves, extra- or non-canonical as they may be, are, whether in Texas or in the Ruhr, real forms of political action in the life of the church. Added to this, the *Decree on the Apostolate of the Laity* declared: "As sharers in the role of Christ the Priest, the Prophet, and the King, the laity have an active part to play in the life and activity of the Church." This indicates (as does the parallel section in the *Dogmatic Constitution on the Church,* which spells this out in greater detail but seems to exclude the laity from the "kingly" function) that the dogmatic shift from a purely hierarchical conception of the church to a more communal one will tend to bolster these democratic political trends. For it would appear that "sharers" in all of the classical christological roles—Priest-Prophet-King—are excluded from nothing as far as responsibility for the total life of the Christian community is concerned. This would obviously include its political life.

Tradition as a matter of fact is in harmony with this modern development. For in the early church, as evidenced from the correspondence of Cyprian (d. 258), the Canons of Hippolytus and the Apostolic Constitutions (representing third-century tradition) and elsewhere, even in the election of the episcopate the laity was involved both in terms of *assent* (confirming the promotion of the most suitable person) and *consent* (agreeing to the election once it had taken place). Cyprian writes that nothing is to be done "without the advice of the clergy and the consent of the laity" (Ep. xiv). By the time of the councils of Orléans (549) and Paris (557) the principle is established: "That a bishop must not be imposed on people against their will" (a quote from Pope St. Celestine I (d. 432). [18] Cyprian, in particular, demands wide consultation, not only with his priests and deacons but also with the people before making decisions (*"nihil sine consilio vestro et sine consensu plebis mea privatim sententia gerere,"* Ep. xiv). Even at the ecumenical councils, from the earliest times, the participation of laity was expected, not in a voting capacity but as advisers and consultants and to give their consent to the decisions reached and to publicize them.

Ironically, as Yves M.-J. Congar notes in his survey of *Lay People in the Church,* this "old tradition. . . wherein the Church spontaneously regulated her life in such a way as actively to involve the whole community, each according to his condition, was brought to an end by powerful laymen abusing their position. . . . Abuses came to such a pass, ecclesiastical affairs were so corrupted by politics, that the Church as far as possible has got rid of all lay connections with episcopal elections." Also, even though laymen participated in varying degrees in the conciliar affairs of the churches in both East and West, and though "the participation of laity, especially of rulers, was regarded as an essential feature of great councils from the Lateran in 1215 to Trent inclusive," the general clericalization of ecclesiastical life was moving toward the exclusion of laymen so that by the time of the Vatican Council of 1869-70 "no lay man was invited thereto, in any capacity whatever."[19]

Julius Cardinal Döpfner, Archbishop of Munich-Freising, one of the leaders of the liberal group at Vatican II, makes two major points in this connection. The first is that as a consequence of the incarnational nature of the church "no concrete form that the Church may take can ever completely express the fullness of the divine life working in her, she must of necessity be able to alter this form if she is to realize her true nature."[20] As he argues, the Chalcedonian christological principle, emphasizing the humanity and historicity of God's involvement in the world, means that the church as human and thus subject to human frailty must always and constantly reform itself: *Ecclesia semper reformanda.*

The second is his concern for greater lay participation in the life of the church. Cardinal Döpfner believes that the words of Pius XII to the laity—"You are the Church!"—have not been "taken nearly seriously enough," either in Catholic ecclesiology or in popular piety. All Christians, through baptism, have a common calling and a common citizenship, and thus also "ruling power." Thus, the Cardinal goes on, though Catholic dogma signifies that the center of government rests with the hierarchy, nevertheless, "throughout history the faithful have in some way shared the responsibility for order in the Church. Even such an authoritarian as Pope Innocent III in the thirteenth century advocated the principle that whatever affected each individual must be sanctioned by common consent."[21]

To combine these two new emphases in the life of the church with its classical dogmatic self-image requires political imagination. As Cardinal Döpfner himself puts it: "The time has come to review some of our old familiar concepts. We cannot continue to hold on to what we have always been used to, merely out of sentiment. . . . We must grow more aware of what is needed today, realizing what is permanent and immutable in the Church, and what can and must be changed if she is to fulfil her mission in the modern world."[22] It is obvious that one of the most critical points is how to combine the "immutable" principle of hierarchical government with the political necessity of full lay participation.

In other words, is the church able to change without changing its essential nature? Is the reconciliation of some of these antinomies between the new ideological forces at work in the church and the classical constitutional patterns impossible? Not if political imagination is fully exercised. One example may be sufficient to indicate what might be done generally in a political *aggiornamento* not only in the Roman Catholic Church but in all churches. In a paper presented to the Canon Law Society of America, Donald P. Warwick—a sociologist and Catholic layman—suggested various structures and procedures to improve organizational effectivness in the Roman Catholic Church. One of his major theses is that "from a practical standpoint there is little doubt that the Roman Catholic Church must increase the degree of lay participation in decision-making if it is to survive." In order to bring about changes in this direction he suggests as a "general guideline that *laymen (male and female) be included in all of the major spheres of decision-making in the Church, including the parish, the diocese, the national conference, the Vatican, and even future ecumenical councils.*"[23] (The italics are Warwick's.)

Can this movement for greater participation of the membership in the government of the church be reconciled with the "immutable" dogmatic principle of hierarchical control and papal supremacy? Warwick believes that it can, and that in two main ways. The first step would be a "radical de-emphasis on the role of the Pope, both in theory and in practice, and a large-scale decentralization of authority." He sees this being accomplished by several means: broadening the base of authority in decision-making, instituting persuasive rather than coercive methods of control over members, re-evaluating the role of the pope theologically, and, the "adoption of a limited term of office for the Pope." As Warwick says, the idea of limiting terms of office has already been applied to appointments to the Curia and if this same principle were operative in regard to the pope "it might have the advantage of providing for younger and more dynamic leadership in the Church. In human terms the College of Cardinals might occasionally vote for a man of 40 if they knew that they could vote him out in 5 or even 10 years."[24]

The second step would be the introduction of "a truly democratic system in which all members have some part in the election of Bishops and the Pope himself." Only in these ways, believes Warwick, will the church remain vital and achieve its true purposes in the context of the overall mission of the Christian people. His principal conclusion is that the Roman Catholic Church must move toward an organizational system "which places much less emphasis upon the papacy, hierarchical authority, clerical prerogatives, and juridical procedures, and which consciously aims at fostering creativity, spontaneity, and freedom in the application of the Gospels to modern life."[25]

What is suggested is basically the application of the Augustinian and Thomistic principle of the mutability of human law to ecclesiastical institutions, customs, and procedures. Thomas Aquinas wrote in response to the question: "Whether human law should be changed in any way?" that "the law can be rightfully changed because of changed conditions among men, to whom different things are expedient according to the difference of their conditions." He is arguing against the static view of law which objects: "That which is right once is right always: therefore, that which is law should always be law." Against this position Thomas quotes Augustine: "On the contrary, Augustine says: 'A temporal law, however just, may be justly changed in the course of time'."[26]

In short, through theological clarification of what are the minimal dogmatic essentials of the church and its government, combined with an imaginative projection of what are the political possibilities for the maximal participation of the total membership, a new form of the church may arise which has integral continuity with the past and also complete identity with the present. Or, to put it another way, what is *right* for the church to be the church has to be combined with what is *expedient* (in Aquinas' sense) for the church to be the church today. The art of church politics is to harmonize effectively these polarities in a living way. It is self-evident that this is not a peculiar challenge for the Roman Catholic Church but one which the whole Christian ecumenical community of churches faces throughout the world.

These declarations on the part of church leaders are hopeful signs. Still, one has the melancholic feeling that whereas the general trend in secular politics has been in the direction of greater popular participation in government, the ecclesiastical situation has remained static. As a result, the church represents one of the last major strongholds of oligarchical, monarchical politics in the modern world. There are, of course, many reasons for this, some of which have already been discussed. But perhaps the most important reason for the church's tendency to become organizationally sclerotic and politically reactionary is a simple failure of political imagination. The churches, because of their tendency to confuse magic with religion and to mix totemism with true sacramentalism, have found it difficult to distinguish their external forms from their intrinsic spirit. And so, whether in regard to dogma or architecture or liturgy, the church has been conservative in the sense of being a hoarder rather than conservative in the sense of being a critical conservator. It has been inclined to cling to everything rather than maintaining that which is essential and best.

Thus, in the political realm, the church by conserving the governmental forms of the past, by perpetuating political styles of bygone days, has become organizationally anachronistic and institutionally dysfunctional. B. A. Cortesi, commenting in the *New York Times* on the 1963 election to choose the successor of Pope John, wrote: "The cardinals gather in conclave for what is in the fullest sense of the term a democratic election. This means that they are free before and during the conclave to indulge in all lawful forms of politicking. They can discuss the merits and faults of the various candidates and try to gain adherents for the candidacy of whoever they think is most fit to occupy the chair of St. Peter."[27] As has been said, if the fact of an election is canonically admitted, correlatively, the necessity of a political process is also admitted. The only question then remaining is: What kind of political process? If "all lawful forms of politicking" are permissible for a conclave of cardinals in choosing the pope, are these same political rights not available to the church as a whole in organizing its political life in general? Is there any fundamental reason, canonically or otherwise, why a popular election, with universal suffrage for all adult church members, might not be a more appropriate form of ecclesiastical election for the contemporary world than a conclave of cardinals, or equally antiquated equivalents related to other church offices?

If, as Erich Fromm argues in *The Sane Society,* the major political malaise of modern man is his feeling of alienation from the decision-making and policy-determining bodies of modern technological society and his feeling of political impotence over against both the immense dimensions of mass society and the impenetrability of bureaucratic controls, this sense of alienation is even more poignant in the context of the religious community for it is here—rightly or wrongly—that the adherent expects most in terms of interpretation of the meaning of life and some living experience through community participation in the reality of the religious vision, the wholeness of life, and the solidarity of mankind. When man is refused recognition as a significant "member" of the corporate body and is denied a significant role in the determination of its character and direction, not only he as an individual but the whole society becomes, in Fromm's words, pathologically non-sane.

A vivid illustration of how important popular participation is for the exercise of political leadership is cited by Bill D. Moyers, former assistant to the President: ". . . there are questions on which governments dare not act without evidence of genuine support. When policies and laws outdistance public opinion, or take public opinion for granted, or fail to command respect in the conscience of the people, they lose their 'natural' legitimacy. As with any rootless condition, the democratic experience then becomes infected with malaise. People feel estranged from their government, seemingly powerless to alter the way things are. They may challenge policy, usually in demonstrations, but their chances of changing policy are slim. Their impotence leads either to numbed apathy or, more dangerously, to outright hostility.

"This is what happened over the last twenty-four months in this country as opposition to the war in Viet Nam swelled to an overpowering crescendo. It did not happen, in my opinion, primarily because some people thought the war immoral, and some thought it illegal and some thought it simply unwinnable at an acceptable cost. I think it happened because a majority of people believed the war undemocratic—waged in violation of the tradition of consent which is fundamental to the effective conduct of foreign policy in a free society."[28]

A similar political malaise within the church has become spectacularly evident with the fierce popular protest against Pope Paul's encyclical on birth control. The root of the resistance does not lie so much in direct antagonism to papal authority as in the sense of outrage at the political "style" which it epitomizes. Whatever may have been the Vatican's reasons for not issuing the document as an "infallible" pronouncement, the political fact is that the directive lacked the consent of the people, which is indispensable for authority to become effective. In the words of Moyers, the encyclical lacked its "natural legitimacy." The pope failed to follow the advice of the commission of experts set up to assist him in reaching a decision, though their opinion was directly contrary to his by a substantial majority, and he furthermore apparently completely miscalculated the general antagonism of Catholic popular opinion to his views in this matter in many major centers of ecclesiastical power within the Roman Church. The poster at the Dortmund Congress—"Don't talk about the pill. We take it."—was a visible sign of popular political resistance making an official "authoritative" pronouncement a legal dead-letter.

The resistance against the pope's encyclical was also symptomatic of a new attitude within the Roman Catholic Church which was symbolized by the resignation of the Abbot of Sieg-burg, Dr. Alkuin Heising, as a protest against "the church's authoritarian attitude" and its efforts to suppress attempts to reform it. However much it may be deplored by the Vatican authorities, the demand for participation and for more democratic politics is an irresistible trend, fanned both by the bitter experience of totalitarianism among the older generation and the natural demand for recognition by an effervescent and radical youth. The church, along with all other established institutions, including the state itself, is being reshaped by these massive forces.

R. H. Tawney once observed: "Institutions which have died as creeds sometimes continue, nevertheless, to survive as habits."[29] Despite polities formally representing more democratic traditions, Protestant ecclesiastical officials seem hardly less authoritarian and politically feudalistic in their actual operations than their Roman Catholic equivalents. The Protestant forms of oligarchical control by a power elite, the maneuvers of a hierarchical "top" manipulating the institution for their own benefit, are more disguised and more subtle than their Catholic counterparts—and thus in some ways more dangerous. Protestant hierarchism tends to emerge today in bureaucratic guise—it is gray-flannel rather than clerical-black in shading and thereby less easily distinguishable and identifiable. The modern Protestant church official may have few, if any, of the external trappings of traditional church power; nevertheless, his actual ability to control the lives of those with whom he works, to shape the ecclesiastical structure, and to influence the general ethos of the institution may exceed that of his historical predecessors who, theoretically, had far more authority. Only recently has the investment portfolio of a church body been seen as the existential test of its social and political conscience. And, at a more personal level, though it may be difficult for most Protestant church leaders to suspend, or even reprimand, recalcitrant clerics, it is not difficult for even more effective forms of institutional repression to be exercised in subtle bureaucratic ways. It is difficult, almost impossible, to convict a theological nonconformist of heresy or to excommunicate an organizational rebel on disciplinary grounds in most Protestant churches. But bureaucratically, the same results can be achieved by withholding assignments through which unpopular views might be propagated or by "accidental" omission from committees, delegations, or other outward and visible signs of institutional recognition. Bureaucratically, the Protestant ecclesiastical tyrants don't need to fight, much less martyr, their opponents; all they need to do is to "forget" and thus organizationally bury them. Heresy trials and excommunication proceedings tend to be messy. Scratching a name from a committee or nominating list is much neater as a means of political disposal. In short, what Gibson Winter has called "a national bureau of promotion" may be a far more effective, as well as better-disguised, form of ecclesiastical oligarchism than the traditional hierarchical structures. Today, the executive's pen is likely to be far more powerful than the prelate's crook in achieving and maintaining political domination in the church.

Fortunately, there are signs that the revolt of the constituency against exclusion from political participation is spreading in Protestant as well as Catholic circles. One of the most vivid examples of a Protestant democratic protest was seen in the election of the new general-secretary of the World Council of Churches in 1964-65. The Executive Committee had nominated a candidate for the post at its summer meeting in 1964. But the nomination was so presented to the press as to appear to be a *fait accompli,* over which the Central Committee—the constitutional body for election—had not even the power of veto. A coalition of political forces representing WCC staff members who did not feel they had been adequately consulted by the nominating committee, religious journalists who felt that the procedures were undemocratic, "young Turks" who had long been suspicious of the political methods of the Council's officers, and Central Committee members who objected to the specific nomination as well as those who felt they had been overlooked and dealt with unconstitutionally, resulted in the Central Committee, in Enugu, Nigeria, in 1965, overturning the proposed nomination and, after a bitter, closed-session battle, electing a new candidate.

Though such political revolts and the activization of democratic forces are sometimes embarrassing to individuals who happen to be the focus of attention, and may introduce an element of chaos disruptive of organizational efficiency, on the whole—even taking the possible excesses into account—such movements have tended to vitalize the bodies politic concerned and have helped to bolster the morale of organizations which have suffered from the sagging passivity or anti-institutional hostilities of their membership. Political participation, in other words, may seem to threaten the institutional structures; yet, without such participatory upheavals the structures are doomed to stagnation and will eventually deteriorate from lack of attention and concern on the part of the constituency.

The report in *New Christian* on the World Council of Churches Assembly in Sweden and the indications of the disaffection of the young with anti-democratic structures and procedures of large-scale ecclesiastical assemblies along with their determination to actively participate in and affect the politics of such meetings, may be seen as a kind of microcosm of a general trend toward politicizing the life of the churches from top to bottom. The forms of this political revolution are varied but the basic demand is the same everywhere: support of an institution only on the basis of freely given consent, identification with an institution only on the basis of full participation. Only those religious institutions, causes, and movements which foster rather than inhibit this participatory democratic spirit have any prospect for survival in a post-magical world.

5-*Politicking*

Voting More and Enjoying It Less?

President's Column

.　　.　　.

At the General Convention in October, elections will have to take place for three offices in the Church: President, Vice President, and Secretary.

As I think of the district convention elections and consider the inquiries that have come to me regarding the elections that are to be held in October, I have come to question the effectiveness of our present system of elections. We follow the so-called Roman ballot where the first ballot becomes a nominations ballot.

It is an excellent procedure in small groups where people know one another; but it lacks the facility of eliciting the thinking of the delegates in large assemblies. This is reflected in the strong temptation that has existed in some quarters of the Church to get out promotional material for given candidates.

Why then did the Church write the Roman ballot system into its Bylaws?

The Church eschews the politicking procedures that are used in secular assemblies. It is concerned that under prayer and reflection God's Holy Spirit should be allowed to make His Will known through the voting procedures.

But the Holy Spirit works through people. And people have

1 4 0

to be informed. Pastors will usually know something about fellow pastors who are nominated even though they may not know them well. But the poor laymen, many of whom may be at a convention for the first time, are in a bind.

Clearly, one does not facilitate the Holy Spirit's use of men by placing a stopper on all opportunity for discussion, nor would it help to open the door to buttonholing delegates and the solicitation of votes.

But would it not help much to charge a nominations committee with the responsibility of submitting a carefully selected roster of names (perhaps 7), with an agreed outline of supporting information on each candidate. This could be prepared in advance, duplicated, and distributed when the nominations committee would report. Thereafter, the Roman system we now use could take over.

It would, of course, be necessary that there be good geographical distribution in the membership of the nominations committee. In a district there might be one from each conference and in the general convention, one from each district.

A constitution or bylaw should never be amended to meet a given problem while the issue involved is before a constituency. But if the suggestion that has been made here commends itself to you let me know. . . . [1]

Bishops and Lobbyists Meet in St. Louis

The American bishops of the Roman Catholic Church met last week in the diminishing but splendid isolation that befits the lords of one of the world's last remaining monarchies. The site was the tower of the Chase Park Plaza Hotel in St. Louis, which affords a panoramic view of that part of their domain bearing the name of the prayerful crusader, King Louis IX. Like the bishops themselves, the hotel is a curious mixture of the modern, the neo-classical and the Byzantine. . . .

For the first time several groups of priests and laymen succeeded in doing some lobbying at a bishops' meeting—albeit in a limited fashion. Representatives of the National Association of Laymen, for example, met with some of the bishops one evening to discuss liturgical reform. Another group, priests seeking to lift the mandatory celibacy requirement, were less successful in advancing their case.

Perhaps more significantly, a group of approximately 100 laymen and priests, members of both official and unofficial Catholic organizations, met at a nearby hotel and made no attempt at all to communicate with the bishops. Their separateness itself asserted their right to add the layman's voice to the bishops' voice as speakers for the entire church. In a keynote address to the group, known as the National Committee on Catholic Concerns, the Rev. John MacKenzie, a Biblical scholar, voiced the assumption of those present that a nondemocratic body can no longer presume to speak for the entire church. "I know nothing in canon law," he declared, "that says that a bishop can be more concerned for the church than I."[2]

Seymour Lipset, in his analysis of voting and elections in *Political Man,* says that the act of voting is "only the final stage in a process of paying attention to politics."[3] This is a warning against overestimating the significance not only of the act of voting but of any particular political action, whether in the politics of the church or of any other association. The mere act of voting is not the cure-all for every political ill, the panacea for all political dilemmas. Nevertheless, recognizing the dangers of oversimplifying politics by reducing it to the magical act of casting a ballot, voting is, both symbolically and actually, the crux of politics, the existential moment of truth in political participation. As Bertrand de Jouvenel puts it: "The phenomenon which denotes a democracy is the activity of voting."[4]

One of the striking characteristics about church politics is that though the symbolic ritual of voting is constitutionally guaranteed and generally observed, it is difficult to detect what the political process is that leads up to the vote, or, to put it another way, of what political action it is the "final stage," to borrow Lipset's phrase. In brief, church politics appears to have polling but no politicking. Rival candidates openly competing for votes are not evident. Organized parties with ideological platforms and programs competing against one another for attention and support do not seem to be in the picture. Overt struggles for position and power between individuals and groups are seldom witnessed.

One explanation for this phenomenon is that the real political decisions in church politics are reached before the formal balloting. Thus the vote becomes in effect a ceremonial ritual to confirm the results of the already completed political process. If, for example, only one name is nominated for a position, the popular vote (whatever that may be) is a mere formality: the real election has taken place elsewhere, at another time, by other electors. This type of covert political process corresponds to what Erving Goffman has called the playing of "discrepant roles." The holders of political power in the ecclesiastical structure, the managers of the church machinery, constitute what Goffman calls a "team"; one of the major tasks of the "team," in order to keep power, is that of "information control." That is, "a team must be able to keep its secrets and have its secrets kept." The performance of the team depends on the management of secrets—*dark secrets . . .* facts about a team which it knows and conceals and which are incompatible with the image of self which the team attempts to maintain before its audience . . . *strategic secrets . . .* intentions and capacities of a team which it conceals from its audience in order to prevent them from adapting effectively to the state of affairs the team is planning to bring about . . . *inside secrets . . .* whose possession marks an individual as being a member of a group and helps the group feel separate and different from those individuals who are not 'in the know.'"[5]

It seems to be a generally conceded principle that effective political power depends on the consent of the governed to the political leadership. This consent is given for various reasons. But, in any case, whereas in primitive society consent to political leadership is granted to some extent on the basis of magical, occult assumptions, in modern society the tendency is to give consent to the extent that the subject has himself actively participated in the selection of the political leader and is constantly involved in the ongoing political process. This is, in part at least, what is meant by democracy. That is why the vote, and the election in a more general sense, has such a critical position in modern political life, not only for practical reasons but also for symbolical ones as well. By participating in an election, by casting a ballot, the citizen is determining the political leadership and also, symbolically, committing himself to the outcome of the election. Thus, by voting, a person tries to shape the political power according to his desires, but also, concomitantly, agrees to abide by the results and therefore accepts the real bearer of political power (as determined by the election) as the symbolic seat of authority as well. In church life, however, these principles do not always seem to operate.

The so-called "ecclesiastical" or "Roman" ballot is an illustration of this political ambivalence in the church. The origins of this system of voting (as the alternative word "Roman" might indicate) are obscure, but the process of election of a pope by the College of Cardinals is the modern example with longest historical antecedents. A contemporary Protestant form of this system of balloting is as follows:

"In the election of a President, the following rules shall obtain: on the first ballot all of the votes cast shall be necessary to an election. On the second ballot, three-fourths of all the votes cast shall be necessary to an election. On the third ballot, two-thirds of all the votes cast shall be necessary to an election. If three ballots fail to result in an election, the fourth ballot shall be confined to the two persons who in the third ballot receive the highest number of votes and no vote cast for any other shall be counted. In the fourth ballot a majority of the votes shall elect."[6]

In general, this form of election allows no previous nominations, nor oral nominations from the floor, and once the voting has begun it is not interrupted until the election is completed.

It is not easy to decipher the precise meaning of these procedures. On one hand, it might be interpreted as a system which puts a maximum weight on the common "mind" of an assembly and thus, presumably, provides that openness through which the Holy Spirit is "allowed to make His Will known through the voting procedures." On the other hand, more cynically viewed, the provision for continuous voting without interruption until election, or its counterpart (and probable antecedent) in the Roman practice of literally walling-up the College of Cardinals until the new pope is elected, might be seen as a realistic provision for minimizing the possibilities of outside interference in the elective process (a not unreasonable precaution at some periods in church history), or, at the least, a means of playing down overt politicking in the choice of church officers.

Though the Roman, or ecclesiastical, ballot has been advocated as a "nonpolitical" mode of election, it is evident on closer examination that it is as "political" as any other. For example, the first ballot is basically a nominating ballot. Theoretically this opens nomination to everyone who is technically eligible to be elected to the office and thus, theoretically, is a highly democratic procedure. In fact, however, in large assemblies representing large organizational entities, such a procedure is highly selective in an arbitrary, almost accidental, fashion. Well-known "names"—usually of those either who are already in the upper echelons of the organization or who have been given prominent public exposure through the church or secular press or some other communications medium—are most likely to be nominated. The fact of their public exposure and the reasons for it may have little or nothing to do with their actual qualifications for the office to be filled.

In addition, it has been said: "If there is one characteristic for a democratic system (besides the ballot itself) that is theoretically required, it is the capacity for, and the practice of discussion"; or as another political scientist has put it: "It is as true of the large as of the small society that its health depends on the mutual understanding which discussion makes possible; and that discussion is the only possible instrument of its democratic government."[7] Whatever public discussion positively contributes to the health of the body politic in terms of building up the *esprit de corps* by the feeling of general participation, the lack of discussion in the ecclesiastical ballot system has a definite, negative limitation as a democratic voting procedure. Elective systems which severely limit, or actually exclude, open public discussion and debate about the prospective candidates put a premium on decisions made prior to the election, on secret caucuses pressing certain candidates' causes; or on "deals" in which positions and/or political favors are bartered by the power elite. Furthermore, the ecclesiastical ballot (and its related forms of voting) facilitates the control of a large organization by a small in-group. The political "ins" not only have greater public exposure throughout the membership but they also, by virtue of the offices they hold, are more often in touch with one another and therefore more able to mobilize themselves and to organize their political power in the interests of their concerns or candidates. The deceptive element in all this is, of course, that such "ecclesiastical" political devices as the Roman ballot *appear* to be nonpolitical, particularly to the uninitiated "outsiders." This is especially true in church conventions in which a "nonpolitical" atmosphere is assiduously cultivated.

For the ecclesiastical "team," therefore, the playing of "discrepant roles" has been made easier than for most political groups by the presumed nonpolitical character of their activities as well as by the fact, already mentioned, that the church politician wields unusual power through the magical transference from sacramental to political authority projected on the priest-pastor. Just as his "secret" ritualistic play—his "hocus pocus" (a corruption of the Latin words of institution of the Mass, *Hoc est enim corpus meum*)—is accepted as symbolic of a mysterious realm of power dependent on spiritual resources outside ordinary comprehension and control but to which his "audience" consents, so in his political play the church leader's "hocus pocus" is accepted and given consent because his politics is also subconsciously felt to be "transubstantiated"

—that is, his political power is felt to embody a mysterious presence of divine authority.

Though this political balance and harmonization has been viable in the past, especially in the intimate, small-scale units of ecclesiastical structure such as the congregation, parish, or even diocese, organizational changes are already manifesting themselves in the life of the church, as elsewhere in modern society, which are making these previous political arrangements anachronistic. Thus, the consent which the constituency gave to the previous "secret" politics of the ecclesiastical team, i.e., the clergy and hierarchy in general, is now gradually being withheld. Previously the laity knew their political leaders; the faces of their pastors and bishops were familiar. Now their political leaders are often faceless functionaries, departmental directors and executive secretaries in far-away offices.

The bureaucratization of the church, therefore, creates a political crisis. Large-scale organization may not necessarily breed political demoralization. The politics of "secrecy" may not necessarily be more corrupt in a large-scale bureaucratic structure than in the small, intimate parish-type organization. It is, however, more suspect of being so in the large organism, partly because of its inevitably greater complexity and intricacy and its greater distance from the constituency, all of which contribute to the sense of powerlessness and ignorance of the estranged "populace" over against the politics of the ecclesiastical higher-ups. Furthermore, the bureaucrats do not have the magical aura surrounding the sacramental role of the priest and therefore their political "play" does not share in that kind of transubstantiated mystique which allowed the kind of paternalistic-familial church politics of the past to function relatively effectively.

The increase in the size and complexity of modern institutions, including the churches, makes inevitable greater bureaucratic development. As in so many other sectors of modern society, the "experts" are in control. The managerial elite of the ecclesiastical machines are almost completely beyond popular political control, and, significantly, their political power is almost entirely independent of their clergy status (which most church bureaucrats still maintain). These church managers constitute "teams" which are, politically speaking, self-perpetuating oligarchies and, like their counterparts in business corporations, though they must periodically give account of their activity to their legal owners—at a stockholders' meeting or church convention, as the case may be—they are almost totally independent of political pressures in their operations.

From a political perspective, this centralization of political power in the hands of a bureaucratic elite, isolated from the electorate and insulated against political pressure, is highly dangerous for the welfare of the body politic. Out of this matrix come many of the anti-institutional psychoses making commitment to the church as an organization problematic—especially among the young—for so many today. The seemingly monolithic structural configurations of modern church bureaucracy and the apparently anti-democratic political processes of both local and general church congregations eventually demoralize the constituency. The whole complex seems to argue the futility of participation and the ineffectiveness of possible attempts to change or affect it. The final result of this anti-political evolutionary process is that, however strong the institution may be in terms of possessing a venerable tradition, an impeccable reputation, an efficient organization, a solid financial base—or any of the other non-political attributes of stability and power—without providing real and readily accessible possibilities of political involvement and participation for its members, it eventually loses the consent of the governed, on which legitimization, formally and psychologically, every viable political system depends.

The rise of the "Big Church" raises a crucial political question for the Christian community. Is the church going to be controlled by a small, bureaucratic elite, an oligarchy of managers—the new technological form of clericalism—or is it going to be governed by a politics of participation? In other words, is the church organization of the future going to be bureaucratically closed or politically open?

Only in this perspective may one ask whether or not it is appropriate to issue "promotional material for given candidates," to engage in "politicking procedures," to initiate "buttonholing delegates and the solicitation of votes" in the political life of the church. All these forms of political activity—so common in secular life—may appear novel, and perhaps even shocking, in the ecclesiastical context. But what, in fact, are the alternatives to overt political participation in choosing leaders, in establishing policies, in promoting new programs, in developing new structures for the "Big Church"?

Is it incongruous, in a religious community, for some to announce themselves as rival candidates for a particular office? Is it incongruous for parties representing different positions in regard to the policy and program of the community to be organized and to put forward candidates representing these ideological platforms for official positions which will determine the possibility of these policies and programs being implemented? Is it incongruous for public opinion to be shaped and mobilized in the interests of the general communal welfare by whatever modern instruments of communication are available to those who wish to undertake this crucial political task? Is it incongruous to have local, regional, national, or international elections to fill the offices which the church requires in order to fulfill its traditional functions and purposes? Is it, in short, improper to have politicking in church?

The first unthinking answer from the church community would seem to be "yes." Though politics is implicit in every church constitution, church politics tends to be a taboo subject. Though various types of election are articulated in constitutional documents, very little overt political exercise of these privileges is evidenced. Candidates stand for office, but explicit campaigning is frowned upon. Factions exist, but openly organized political parties are excluded. Political opinions are subtly formed, but direct propaganda is anathematized.

The universal political problem in the life of the church is that church politics does exist but it tends to be unacknowledged and hidden. And, as is so often true when politics is denied overt expression, it is more than likely that kind of politics which serves the interest and maintains the power of those who already have the political control. One need not be unduly cynical to recognize the truth of Bertrand Russell's comment already noted in regard to the paradox of church politics as it can be observed in the history of Christianity, namely, the way in which "superior virtue is used as a means of winning tyrannical power for an organization." As Russell points out, the problem of political power and its responsible use and popular control is particularly difficult in the church because "an organization which has ideal ends . . . therefore [has] an excuse for love of power."[8]

That moral superiority corrupts absolutely is an exaggeration. Yet, there is a kernel of truth in the idea that an organization with a reputation for moral virtue is less likely to be critically scrutinized and therefore is granted greater political laxity than other bodies. For this reason, among others, it may be argued that church politics has a greater potential for becoming corrupt than secular politics. This is not only because the general public or the particular constituency is inclined to give religious organizations and leaders the benefit of the doubt in respect to their intentions and motives but also because, psychologically, sincere but misguided religious passions may lead to genuine self-deception in political matters. The ethical view that the end justifies the means is, of course, particularly congenial to those having an unwavering and fanatical conviction of the absolute virtue of the ends sought.

Besides, as John Stuart Mill stated as a political commonplace in *Considerations on Representative Government* (1861), it is fallacious to assume that personal virtues exhibited in private will be maintained by that person when he attains political power: "This is the meaning of the universal tradition, grounded on universal experience, of men's being corrupted by power.

Every one knows how absurd it would be to infer from what a man is or does when in a private station, that he will be and do exactly the like when a despot on a throne; where the bad parts of his human nature, instead of being restrained and kept in subordination by every circumstance of his life and by every person surrounding him, are courted by all persons, and ministered to by all circumstances. It would be quite as absurd to entertain a similar expectation in regard to a class of men; the Demos, or any other. Let them be ever so modest and amenable to reason while there is a power over them stronger than they, we ought to expect a total change in this respect when they themselves become the strongest power."[9]

The traditional familial ethos of the church, with such emotionally charged domestic imagery as "mother church" assiduously cultivated, makes such a realistic assessment of human nature and the impact upon it of power and the political environment appear out of place and inappropriate. Yet if nothing else, the growth of the church—whether in its Protestant or Roman Catholic form—into large-scale bureaucracies and huge political complexes makes such observations as those of Mill highly relevant to the present problems of church politics. In a small religious association, the intimate connection between the members and the leaders, the open channels of communication, and the unanimity of purpose, make the political life of the group simple and straightforward. But as the group becomes larger, more ideologically diverse, less homogeneous, and increasingly multilayered in structure, church politics takes on some of the complexities that plague bigness in all organization. Increasing size means increasing depersonalization of the political process in a religious organization. And it is under these circumstances, an irreversible trend in modern life, that some of the same safeguards for the political health of the community need to be instituted in the church as have been found necessary in secular society in its struggle to achieve and maintain representative and responsible government.

The Roman Catholic Church may appear to have a monopoly on problems having to do with authoritarian and over-centralized power and ingrown political processes, i.e., the popes select the cardinals and the cardinals elect the popes. In Protestantism, however, the same phenomena may be observed. Kenneth Boulding has cited several "iron laws" in organizational development. One of these is "the iron law of hierarchy" and it means: "The larger the organization, the more elaborate will be its hierarchical structure, the more grades there will be in it, and the greater is likely to be the difficulty of direct communication between the lower and upper grades."[10] Partly through natural growth and partly through ecumenical consolidation, the major Protestant churches have become large-scale organizations in which the iron law of hierarchy is fully operative with all of the attendant political problems which that entails.

Harvey Cox argues that the bureaucratization of religious organizations and the concomitant "managerial revolution" that it has provoked means the emergence of a "New Breed" of church leaders who, "despite explicit doctrines of congregational autonomy and grass-roots authority . . . form and lead rather than merely reflect the opinions of their constituencies."[11] However, this revolution which has "freed ministers and church executives from subservience to laymen" can also create political backlash. As Milton Yinger has written: "Policy-making is likely to be 'delegated upward'—to national or international conventions, composed of those persons most concerned with the problem in hand. But many kinds of action are of necessity 'delegated downward'—to local churches and individuals." Needless to say, it is often easier to get international or national consensus on policy than local action and implementation. Therefore, as Yinger also notes, there are many "paper victories" won at denominational or ecumenical conventions which create feelings of exhilaration and achievement. Later, however, the minority responsible for the agreements reached discover they have underestimated the apathy and opposition of the nonparticipating majority, they discover they "have been misled by what Robert Merton has called 'the fallacy of group soliloquy'—the feeling of unanimity

reached by a small minority unmindful of their relative isolation."[12]

The most vivid historical example of this is found in the
fate of the Orthodox participants in the Council of Florence
(1438 - 39) who on returning home were stoned in the streets
of Constantinople by irate laity because of the conciliatory
agreements they had made with the Roman Church in the interests of Christian unity. Delegates to ecumenical conferences
or representatives at church union negotiations today are not
likely to suffer as dramatic consequences for their actions,
but the fact remains that political nonparticipation on the part
of the vast majority of the churches breeds organizational backlash and a general political malaise.

Thus when such a group as the National Committee on
Catholic Concerns asserts that "a non-democratic body can
no longer presume to speak for the entire church" they are
not saying that church politicians are worse than secular politicians but only just as good. When Father MacKenzie declares
that he knows of "nothing in canon law that says that a bishop
can be more concerned for the church than I," he is not im-
pugning anyone's morals or motives but simply affirming the
common political responsibility of all members for the well-
being of the Christian commonwealth, and further affirming
that the political structures of the past are inadequate to cope
with the political realities of today.

"Governments must be made for human beings as they are,"
John Stuart Mill said; thus a "certain amount of conscience,
and of disinterested public spirit, may fairly be calculated
on in the citizens of any community ripe for representative
government." Without this sense of essential human dignity,
of course, the very idea of democracy would be absurd. "But
it would be ridiculous," adds Mill, "to expect such a degree
of it, combined with such intellectual discernment, as would
be proof against any plausible fallacy tending to make that
which was for their class interest appear the dictate of justice
and of the general good."[13]

It is on the basis of these realistic assumptions about indi-

vidual and group behavior that Mill's argumentation for democratic structures and processes is based. Mill writes: "One of
the greatest dangers, therefore, of democracy, as of all other
forms of government, lies in the sinister interest of the holders of power: it is the danger of class legislation, of government
intended for (whether really effecting it or not) the immediate benefit of the dominant class, to the lasting detriment of
the whole. And one of the most important questions demanding consideration, in determining the best constitution of a
representative government, is how to provide efficacious se-
curities against this evil."[14]

It may appear that this analysis is irrelevant to most forms
of church politics. As has been suggested, however, it would
be naïve to assume that there is nothing equivalent to "the
sinister interest of the holders of power" or the "danger of class
legislation" in church affairs. Whereas a church official is not
likely to be "sinister" in a malicious sense, it is not unlikely
that he may be "left-handed" in a psychological sense—that
is, in seeking and finding psychic satisfaction in positions of
power and status within the church without really admitting
these drives and motivations to himself. For example, in one
recent ecumenical gathering, the incumbent officeholders expressed chagrin at political activities initiated to encourage
open "electioneering," on the grounds that such "politicking"
was beneath the dignity of a church conclave and that this
kind of overt political action was inappropriate for a religious
body. What they did not seem to realize—and this is psychologically their "sinister" blind spot—is that an incumbent, even
in an open election, has the advantage of constant public exposure plus the natural conservative inertia of the electorate to
give him an almost unsurmountable headstart in the campaign
for office. In other words, "no politics" is the strongest political guarantee for the perpetuation of the *ancien regime* and
the most solid base for the continuation of the political establishment.

Modern psychological perspectives and insights have also
made the meaning of the "danger of class legislation" in church

politics more transparent than hitherto. Blatant clericalism is no longer the political threat to the welfare of the church that it once was. As has been indicated, this kind of sacerdotal despotism by a clerical elite is on the wane in most churches. Nevertheless, a new form of clerical domination has arisen—that of bureaucratic control through bureaus, offices, departments, and other "curial" structures of ecclesiastical organization. Clerk and cleric have a common etymology. Though traditional clericalism has been closely associated with liturgical and cultic supremacy and from that sacerdotal-magical complex broadened into political domination, the control of church politics by clergy elites of one sort or another has also derived from the more purely bureaucratic power of the "clerks" who run the ecclesiastical, legal, and administrative machinery.

Once again, it must be noted that the increase in the size and complexity of the operations of the churches and the concomitant development of increasingly large bureaucratic structures inevitably involves a shifting of power centers within the political life of these religious bodies. The "nonpolitical" bureaucrat may in fact have more political power and influence than those nominally elected, and therefore "political" figures in the ecclesiastical institution. The Protestant church president, for example, may have the formal supremacy and status; the departmental heads may have the actual political control of the organization. The Roman Catholic pope may have the canonical authority; the curial officials may have the bureaucratic power and therefore real political supremacy.

To return again to the idea that voting is "only the final stage in a process," the reformation of church politics not only must center on making the vote itself more significant but also must address itself to the revitalization of the whole political process which leads up to the vote and continues beyond it. Some immediate first steps might be taken:

First, the voting age ought to be lowered in the church. This, of course, is a general political trend. However, the arguments are particularly strong in church politics. Erik Erikson and other behavioral and social scientists have commented on the social and psychological dislocations that are being caused by the prolonged isolation of adolescents from adult society and the "scarring" (as Bruno Bettelheim calls it) of personality, individual and social, that results from the "conflicts between a youth either afraid of or prevented from coming into its own and an older generation unwilling or unable to give way," in our modern culture.[15] The same kind of impasse can exist in the church when the younger generation is not given its political rights when it has long since become aware of its political power, or is paternalistically segregated, and thus politically neutralized, in so-called youth departments. If confirmation (or adult baptism in those churches practicing it) could be reinterpreted as the rite of political as well as sacramental adulthood, it would take on new meaning and significance in the Christian community. Thus, confirmation would not only, as in the past, grant full sacramental privileges but would also grant full political privileges, in terms of voting rights as well as the right to hold office. Combining the sacramental and political initiation would in itself be significant, for it would symbolize the harmonious unity of all elements of the church's life necessary for its existence and for it to fulfull its mission to the world.

The second step would be to encourage overt political campaigning for ecclesiastical offices. In part this is necessary to provide the whole membership of the church the chance of choosing among different candidates for office. The purpose here would not be to foster personality contests, but, rather, since each candidate would presumably campaign on the basis of certain policies and programs which he and his supporters advocate, to allow the church at large to express its view of past and future directions of church life. In other words, not only would a popularly elected church official have the authority of freely given consent by the electorate, but also the election itself would provide a forum for the public opinion of the Christian community to be informed and articulated.

As Pope Pius XII said at a Catholic press congress at Rome in 1950: "Public opinion is the attribute of every society made up of men who, conscious of their personal and social behaviour, are closely concerned in the community of which they are members. . . . In the eyes of every Christian, to stifle the citizens' voice and force them to be silent is an outrage of man's natural right, a violation of the order of the world as God has established it. . . . We wish, too, to add a word about public opinion within the Church herself (concerning those matters, of course, that are open to free discussion). This can surprise only those who do not know the Church or know her insufficiently. She is a living body, and something would be lacking to her life were there no public opinion in it, a want for which the blame would rest on pastors and faithful."[16]

A third consideration in setting up elections to serve as this kind of public opinion forum for the church is that the cooperation of the church press would be required. A free church press is a prerequisite for political democracy in the church, for a controlled "company paper" would consciously or unconsciously be an instrument in the hands of the ecclesiastical establishment. Each major candidate (to be determined by some equivalent of the primary system in state and national politics) would be ensured full and equal opportunity, (including, of course, those incumbents in office seeking re-election) to inform the electorate of his views and to set forward his proposed policies and programs.

As a fourth step, it would also probably be necessary for the church to provide some kind of financial subsidy to defray some of the costs incurred by the candidates in their campaign for office. In the present situation, the incumbents in church offices are provided a free platform for their campaign for re-election and are, in fact, subsidized by the church in their political activities, since they are on church salary and their functional activities cannot easily be separated from their purely political endeavors, however sincerely they may seek to avoid this overlapping of roles.

These are procedural suggestions, but fundamental to a

reformation of church politics is the clear differentiation between those offices in the church which are basically political and those which are administrative and thus bureaucratic. The administrative functionaries ought to be provided the security of the equivalent of civil service tenure. This provides continuity for the essential organizational operations of the church and also makes it possible to require of such administrative cadres political neutrality. In other words, insofar as legal provision and common consent can achieve this, the political life of the church ought to be protected from the encroachment of bureaucratic power.

It is obvious that the major offices of the religious organization are political, for example, the president and the vice-president of a national church body, the chief pastor in a congregation, the president of an ecumenical organization such as the World Council of Churches or the National Council of Churches, or the bishop in a church with episcopal polity. These are fairly obvious political posts which ought to be filled by democratic political processes and be held responsible by regular political checks and balances.

The major power posts in the bureaucratic and administrative structure of the church present a more complicated political dilemma. To some extent these positions are policy-making and not simply administrative in function. Departmental heads, or their equivalent, are the most clear case in point. Should they be tenured, nonpolitical, civil service appointments, or should they be elective and thus political positions? As has been pointed out, some of these officials, who are only technical functionaries in theory, can and have become powerful political forces in a religious organization, with powers totally incommensurate with the administrative rank they possess. In one church it is said to be the main finance officer. In another, the secretary of the Board of Foreign Missions is considered the most powerful political figure in the church, even though it is a body with episcopal polity.

This common confusion between politics and bureaucracy in the churches strongly argues for corrective measures, perhaps the creation of some unprecedented political form in church life equivalent to the party system in secular politics. Party politics might be considered antithetical to the nature and purposes of the Christian fellowship. On the other hand, overt and rationally structured "partisanship" might be considered a political expression of the "diversity of gifts" in the Christian body. Open campaigns for elective offices, frank public discussion of controversial issues, and free competitive efforts to shape the public opinion of the church would all be consistent with an ecclesiastical party system in church political life.

But a party system in politics has another major constructive function besides providing the means for open confrontation and debate on critical and controversial issues regarding the policy and program of the community. A party striving for political power is also, by implication, offering to fill the major policy-making positions with those who are representatives of the major ideological and programatic thrusts of the party. Thus, in the British parliamentary system, for example, the "loyal opposition" (which already implies the constructive purposes of a party out of power, or indeed the need for political opposition for the political wholeness of a people) has a "shadow cabinet." This cabinet is made up of those who, within their own party circles, have been provisionally nominated to fill the actual cabinet posts should their party become the government.

Though it is clear that such analogies between different institutions may not be pursued to extremes, yet the equivalent of a British or American cabinet member may be increasingly necessary as religious organizations become larger and more complicated and more bureaucratically oriented. For a cabinet minister, or officer, is, though not elective, a political man. His position is dependent on the party in power, and he remains in his position only so long as his party is the government. One of the protections against complete bureaucratic compartmentalization in government is the politically appointed cabinet member. So, religious organizations, as they become more and more bureaucratic, may find it necessary to create the equivalent of "cabinet ministers" to act as chiefs of the major departments of the ecclesiastical organization.

Walter Bagehot writes of the values of this system of constant "changes of ministry" in the British system: "As soon as we take the true view of Parliamentary office we shall perceive that fairly frequent change in the official is an advantage, not a mistake. If his function is to bring a representative of outside sense and outside animation in contact with the inside world, he ought often to be changed. . . . If the function of a Parliamentary minister is to be an outsider to his office, we must not choose one who, by habit, thought, and life, is acclimatized to its ways. . . . This conception of the use of a Parliamentary head shows how wrong is the obvious notion which regards him as the principal administrator of his office. The late Sir George Lewis used to be fond of explaining this subject. He had every means of knowing. He was bred in the permanent civil service. He was a very successful Chancellor of the Exchequer, a very successful Home Secretary, and he died Minister for War. He used to say, 'It is not the business of a Cabinet Minister to work his department. His business is to see that it is properly worked. If he does much, he is probably doing harm. The permanent staff of the office can do what he chooses to do much better, or if they cannot, they ought to be removed. He is only a bird of passage, and cannot compete with those who are in the office all their lives round.' Sir George Lewis was a perfect Parliamentary head of an office, so far as that head is to be a keen critic and rational corrector of it."[17]

One sees in this institution the practical wisdom (as in so many other areas of British politics) of setting political and bureaucratic powers over against one another. As Bagehot observes, the perfect bureaucratic system is one which fulfills Voltaire's definition of "the art of government. . . to make two-thirds of a nation pay all it possibly can pay for the benefit of the other third." In other words, the bureaucratic mentality tends to confuse the maintenance of government structure with the social purposes that structure is intended to meet. It is the purpose of politics to correct the bureaucracy, to reign supreme over it, and harness it for its true political ends. Thus, the "cabinet minister" in the new age of ecclesiastical bureacracy could achieve what his counterpart in secular politics is intended for: "There is every reason to expect that a Parliamentary statesman will be a man of quite sufficient intelligence, quite enough various knowledge, quite enough miscellaneous experience, to represent effectually general sense in opposition to bureaucratic sense."[18]

The greatest political test facing the church of today may be, therefore, as it was in secular politics at the time of Mill, "between a representative democracy and a bureaucracy: all other governments may be left out of account." The most crucial dilemma facing the church in its organizational life may be to find that kind of politics which can bring these two polar forces into harmonious relation with one another. Without skilled bureaucratic administration and organization, the church can neither survive in nor minister to the modern technological world. But without popular political participation in its government, the church will cease to have members who are in any vital relation to it. Mill puts the issue well: "There could not be a moment's hesitation between representative government, among a people in any degree ripe for it, and the most perfect imaginable bureaucracy. But it is, at the same time, one of the most important ends of political institutions, to attain as many of the qualities of the one as are consistent with the other; to secure, as far as they can be made compatible, the great advantage of the conduct of affairs by skilled persons, bred to it as in intellectual profession, along with that of a general control vested in, and seriously exercised by, bodies representative of the entire people."[19]

It is this distinction—in essence, in Mill's words, of "recognizing the line of separation . . . between the work of government properly so called, which can only be well performed after special cultivation, and that of selecting, watching, and, when needful, controlling the governors, which in this case, as in all others, properly devolves, not on those who do the work, but on those for whose benefit it ought to be done"[20] — which has been almost totally ignored in canon law, as well as in traditional ecclesiological treatments of church order. It is the distinction between administration and politics. And because church politics has not been recognized as a distinct sphere, with its own integrity and its own rationale, the government of the church has been left almost entirely to the bureaucrats, who operate according to the precepts and conventions of the status quo and to that extent are insensitive to and incapable of responding to those dynamic and unpredictable forces of renewal and change which can, if they are allowed and given constructive direction, constantly reform and reshape the church. This is the peculiar province of church politics. It is that high calling which gives church politics its dignity and integrity and which makes it for those who commit themselves to it not only an art and a science but also a spiritual vocation.

Postlude

Nine and Five Theses

Principles

1. The church is both a spiritual fellowship *(koinonia)* and a political institution *(ekklesia)*.
2. Church politics, like secular politics, has to do with the distribution of power, and responsibility for it.
3. The same political dynamics and processes characteristic of human social institutions are found in the church's political life.
4. The same scientific resources available for analyzing other political institutions and processes are also applicable in studying church politics.
5. The similarity between church politics and other forms of politics has tended to be denied and camouflaged in the church: however, this repression and denial of politics in the church has not done away with the political problems inherent in church life but has made them more difficult to define and handle.
6. The ultimate political authority of the church is vested in the whole body, the people of God, and they are in common responsible for the welfare of the corporation; the appropriate form of government for the church is, therefore, democratic, with all full members having equal political rights, privileges, and opportunities.

163

7. The power of the ballot and universal suffrage is the heart of the democratic system; when exercise of the ballot is relinquished, either formally or effectively, to an elite few, or to a bureaucratic clique, the politics tends to become self-perpetuating and static, insensitive to changing needs and desires of the people.
8. To preserve or reclaim for the church the vitalizing function of universal suffrage, political activity should be legitimized and encouraged.
9. The constitutional forms of church government are shaped and determined by the functions of the Christian community, and the style of church politics follows from the nature of the Christian message and the needs of the Christian community.

Proposals

1. The vote should be conferred on every church member at the time of confirmation. The rite of confirmation would thus involve the granting of full political as well as sacramental privileges in the church.
2. Political officials and bureaucratic functionaries should be clearly distinguished in church law. Political positions should be filled through ordinary political processes, including public campaigns for office by the candidates, public discussion of the issues, the issuance of public statements of positions by candidates for office on major issues facing the church, and popular election.
3. The organization of political parties or caucuses should be encouraged as a means of facilitating political action and encouraging basic ideological confrontation and clarification in the church.
4. A free church press should be guaranteed by making it an independent trust, free from political or bureaucratic influence or control, and it should be charged with the responsibility of providing an open forum for political debate on issues as well as a platform for candidates for political office in the church.

5. A bill of rights should be formulated to guarantee the democratic privileges and secure the legal rights of all members of the church.

Notes

Chapter 1. PSYCHEDELICS

1. *Chicago Sun-Times,* January 20, 1968.
2. "Dogmatic Constitution on the Church," *Documents of Vatican II,* ed. Walter M. Abbott, trans. ed. Joseph Gallagher (New York: The American Press, Angelus Books, 1966), p. 70.
3. Ibid., p. 22.
4. Karl Rahner, "Christians in the Modern World," in *Mission and Grace,* I, ed. Rahner (London: Sheed and Ward, Stag Books, 1963), p. 11.
5. Ibid., p. 31.
6. James G. Frazer, *The Golden Bough,* 1-vol. abridged ed. (New York: The Macmillan Company, 1922), p. 55.
7. E. O. James, *Christian Myth and Ritual* (New York: The World Publishing Company, Meridian Books, 1965), p. 305.
8. Bronislaw Malinowski, *Freedom and Civilization* (Bloomington: Indiana University Press, 1960), p. 214.
9. Reinhold Niebuhr, *Essays in Applied Christianity* (New York: Meridian Books, 1959), p. 199.
10. Ernst Cassirer, *An Essay on Man* (New Haven, Conn.: Yale University Press, 1944), pp. 136-142 *passim.*
11. A. A. Brill, *Basic Principles of Psychoanalysis* (New York: Washington Square Press, 1960), p. 36.
12. C. S. Hall, *Primer of Freudian Psychology* (New York: New American Library, Mentor Books, 1954), pp. 79, 82, 83.
13. Ibid., p. 79.
14. Ibid., pp. 82-83.

15. Plato, *The Republic,* trans. H. D. P. Lee (London: Faber & Faber, Penguin Books, 1955). From the Introduction by Lee, p. 14.

16. George Bernard Shaw, *Fabian Essays in Socialism* (Garden City, N.Y.: Doubleday & Company, Dolphin Books; originally published London, 1889), pp. 214, 216, 217.

17. C. P. Snow, *Variety of Men* (New York: Charles Scribner's Sons, 1967), pp. 166, 168.

18. *Berkeley* (Calif.) *Daily Gazette,* July, 1968.

19. Herbert Read, *The Meaning of Art* (London: Faber & Faber, Pelican Books, 1949), p. 191.

Chapter 2. POLITY

1. *Berkeley* (Calif.) *Daily Gazette,* July, 1968.

2. *San Francisco Chronicle,* July, 1968.

3. Ernst Cassirer, *Language and Myth* (New York: Harper & Brothers, 1946), p. 90.

4. Ibid., pp. 91-94.

5. Ibid., pp. 90-91.

6. G. M. Carter and J. H. Herz, *Government and Politics in the Twentieth Century* (New York: Frederick A. Praeger, 1961), p. 3.

7. Eduard Schweizer, *Church Order in the New Testament* (Chicago: Allenson, 1961), Part I, 1a.

8. Ibid., 2m.

9. Kenneth Kirk, ed., *Apostolic Ministry* (London: Hodder and Stoughton, 1946), p. 550.

10. Edwin Hatch, *The Organization of the Early Christian Churches* (London, 1881).

11. T. M. Lindsay, *The Church and the Ministry in the Early Centuries,* 2nd ed. (London: Hodder and Stoughton, 1903), p. 121.

12. Ernest F. Scott, *The Nature of the Early Church* (New York: Charles Scribner's Sons, 1941), p. 110.

13. Lindsay, *The Church and the Ministry,* p. 356.

14. J. B. Lightfoot, *Dissertations on the Apostolic Age* (London: Macmillan and Co., 1892), p. 137.

15. Scott, *Early Church,* p. 110.

16. C. H. Turner, *Studies in Early Church History* (London: Oxford University Press, 1912), p. 35.

17. B. H. Streeter, *The Primitive Church* (London: Macmillan and Co., 1930), p. 261.

18. Scott, *Early Church,* pp. 111-114.

19. Lightfoot, *Apostolic Age,* p. 137.

20. Scott, *Early Church,* p. 112.

21. Lightfoot, *Apostolic Age,* p. 203. Cf. Adolf Harnack *The Mission and Expansion of Christianity in the First Three Centuries* (New York: Williams and Norgate, 1908), p. 437.

22. Martin Luther, "To the Christian Nobility of the German Nation Concerning the Reform of the Christian Estate" (1520), in *Luther's Works* (Philadelphia: Fortress Press, 1966), 44:133, 136.

23. Martin Marty, Review of *The Faith of a Heretic,* in *Christian Century,* November 29, 1961.

24. H. M. Ruitenbeck, ed., *The Dilemma of Organizational Society* (New York: E. P. Dutton, 1963).

25. Harland Cleveland, "Case for Bureaucracy: Exposing Six 'Myths,'" *New York Times,* November 1, 1967.

26. Frank Lloyd Wright, *Writings and Buildings,* ed. Edgar Kaufmann and Ben Raeburn (New York: Horizon Press, 1960), p. 313.

27. *Consultation on Church Union,* (Cincinnati: Forward Movement Press, 1967), p. 128.

28. Hans Küng, *The Council and Reunion* (London: Sheed and Ward, Stag Books, 1961), pp. 188-190.

29. Ibid., p. 191.

30. Ibid., p. 195.

31. *Consultation on Church Union,* pp. 127-128.

32. W. J. J. Gordon, *Synectics* (New York: Harper & Row, 1961), pp. 6-7.

33. Ibid., pp. 128-129.

34. Ibid., pp. 158-159.

35. Wright, *Writings and Buildings,* pp. 91-92.

36. Ibid., p. 93.

37. Alfred North Whitehead, "Uses of Symbolism,," in Rollo May, ed., *Symbolism in Religion and Literature* (New York: George Braziller, 1960), pp. 249-250.

38. R. Buckminster Fuller, "The Age of Astro-Architecture," *Saturday Review,* July 13, 1968, p. 17.

Chapter 3. POWER

1. *The Times* (London), August 14, 1968.

2. *San Francisco Chronicle,* July, 1968.

3. Ibid., July, 1968.

4. Ibid., July 1, 1968.

5. Norbert Wiener, *The Human Use of Human Beings: Cybernetics and Society* (Garden City, N.Y.: Doubleday & Company, Anchor Books, 1954), p. 61.

6. Hans Kung, *The Changing Church* (London: Sheed and Ward, Stag Books, 1965), pp. 147-148.

7. Ibid., p. 85.

8. Christopher S. Wren, "Black Power Shakes the White Church," *Look,* January 7, 1969, p. 84.

9. Irving Howe, *Politics and the Novel* (New York: Horizon Press, 1957), pp. 221-222.

10. Bertrand de Jouvenel, *On Power: Its Nature and the History of Its Growth,* trans. J. F. Huntington (Boston: Beacon Press, 1962), p. 17.

11. Bertrand Russell, *Power: A New Social Analysis* (London: Allen and Unwin, 1960), pp. 9-10.

12. Newton Flew, *The Idea of Perfection in Christian Theology* (New York: Humanities Press, 1968; originally published 1929), p. 275.

13. Reinhold Niebuhr, *Christian Realism and Political Problems* (New York: Charles Scribner's Sons, 1953), p. 149.

14. V. I. Lenin, "What Is to Be Done? Burning Questions of Our Movement," *Marx, Engels, Marxism,* 4th Eng. ed. (Moscow: Foreign Language Publishing House, 1951), p. 135.

15. Lenin, "The Tasks of the Youth Leagues," ibid., pp. 534-535.

16. Paul Tillich, *Love, Power, and Justice* (New Oxford University Press, Galaxy Books, 1954), pp. 37-40.

17. Martin Luther, "On the Councils and the Church" (1539), in *Luther's Works* (Philadelphia: Fortress Press, 1966), 44:173-175.

18. Ibid.

19. Tillich, *Love, Power, and Justice,* pp. 119-120.

20. Anthony Storrs, *Human Aggression* (New York: Atheneum, 1968), pp. 109, 57.

21. Cf. Perrin Stryker, "How to Treat Vice Presidents," in *The Executive Life,* by the Editors of *Fortune* (Garden City, N.Y.: Doubleday & Company, Dolphin Books, 1956), pp. 153 ff.

22. Roy Lewis and Rosemary Stewart, *The Managers: A New Examination of the English, German, and American Executive* (New York: New American Library, Mentor Books, 1958), p. 246.

23. Quoted in ibid., p. 249.

24. Ibid.

25. Niebuhr, *The World Crisis and American Responsibility* (New York: Association Press, 1958), pp. 55-56.

26. Russell, *Power,* p. 49.

27. Niebuhr, *Christian Realism,* p. 11.

28. Niebuhr, *Man's Nature and His Communities* (New York: Charles Scribner's Sons, 1965), pp. 52, 51.

29. Storrs, *Human Aggression,* pp. 121-122.

30. Erich Fromm, *Sigmund Freud's Mission* (New York: Harper & Brothers, 1959), pp. 83 ff.

Chapter 4. PARTICIPATION

1. *San Francisco Chronicle,* July, 1968.
2. Ibid., July, 1968.
3. "Spotlight on Uppsala," *New Christian,* July 25, 1968, p. 8.
4. Bertrand de Jouvenel, *On Power: Its Nature and the History of its Growth,* trans. J. F. Huntington (Boston: Beacon Press, 1962), p. 73.
5. Walter Bagehot, *The English Constitution* (Garden City, N.Y.: Doubleday & Company, Dolphin Books; originally published 1872), pp. 127-128.
6. Harold Laski, *Politics* (Philadelphia: J. B. Lippincott, 1932), pp. 81-82.
7. George H. Williams, "The Ministry of the Ante-Nicene Church," in H. Richard Niebuhr and Daniel Day Williams, eds., *The Ministry in Historical Perspectives* (New York: Harper & Brothers, 1956), p. 49.
8. Roland H. Bainton, "The Ministry in the Middle Ages," in Niebuhr and Williams, *The Ministry,* pp. 90-91.
9. Stanislaus Woywod, *A Practical Commentary on the Code of Canon Law,* rev. and enl. ed., rev. Callistus Smith (New York: Joseph F. Wagner, 1962), p. 107.
10. *New York Times,* February 10, 1969.
11. Reinhold Niebuhr, *Christian Realism and Political Problems* (New York: Charles Scribner's Sons, 1953), p. 96.
12. Jerome Frank, *Law and the Modern Mind* (Garden City, N.Y.: Doubleday & Company, Anchor Books, 1963), p. 344.
13. Xavier Rynne, *Letters from Vatican City* (New York: Farrar, Straus & Giroux, 1963), p. 8.
14. Karl Rahner and Joseph Ratzinger, *The Episcopate and the Primacy* (Montreal: Palm Publishers, 1962), p.14.
15. Hans Küng, *Structures of the Church* (New York: Thomas Nelson, 1964), p. 258.
16. Rahner, *Bishops: Their Status and Function,* trans. Edward Quinn (Baltimore: Helicon Press, 1964), p. 26.
17. Walter M. Abbott, ed., *The Documents of Vatican II,* trans. ed. Joseph Gallagher (New York: The American Press, Angelus Books, 1966), pp. 548-549.
18. Yves M.-J. Congar, *Lay People in the Church* (New York: Newman Press, 1964; originally published London, 1957), p. 233.

19. Ibid., pp. 233-234, 237.

20. Julius Cardinal Döpfner, *The Questioning Church,* trans. Barbara Waldstein (Westminster, Md.: Newman Press, 1964), p. 21.

21. Ibid., pp. 52-53.

22. Ibid., p. ix.

23. In James A. Coriden, ed., *We, the People of God: A Study of Constitutional Government for the Church* (Huntington, Ind.: Our Sunday Visitor, Inc., 1968), pp. 107ff.

24. Ibid.

25. Ibid.

26. Thomas Aquinas, *Summa Theologica,* Q. 97, Art. 2.

27. *New York Times,* June 12, 1963.

28. Bill D. Moyers. "One Thing We Learned," *Foreign Affairs,* vol. 46, no. 4 (July 1968).

29. R. H. Tawney, *Equality* (New York: G. P. Putnam's Sons, Capricorn Books, 1951), p. 20.

Chapter 5. POLITICKING

1. Fredrick A. Schiotz (President, The American Lutheran Church), in *Commentator,* August 1966, p. 4.

2. Edward B. Fiske, *New York Times,* April 28, 1968.

3. Seymour Lipset, *Political Man* (Garden City, N.Y.: Doubleday & Company, Anchor Books, 1963), p. 185.

4. Bertrand de Jouvenel, *On Power: Its Nature and the History of Its Growth,* trans. J. F. Huntington (Boston: Beacon Press, 1962), p. 268.

5. Erving Goffman, *The Presentation of Self in Everyday Life* (Garden City, N.Y.: Doubleday & Company, Anchor Books, 1959), p. 141.

6. Minutes of the First Convention of the United Lutheran Church in America, 1917.

7. B. R. Berelson, P. F. Lazarsfeld, and W. N. McPhee, *Voting: A Study of Opinion Formation in a Presidential Campaign* (Chicago: University of Chicago Press, 1954); quoted in Michael Curtis, ed., *The Nature of Politics* (New York: Avon Books, 1962), p. 519.

8. Bertrand Russell, *Power: A New Social Analysis* (London: Allen and Unwin, 1960), p. 49.

9. John Stuart Mill, *Considerations on Representative Government* (Chicago: Henry Regnery, 1962; originally published London, 1861), p. 133.

10. Kenneth Boulding, *The Organizational Revolution* (New York: Harper & Brothers, 1953), p. 79.

11. Harvey Cox, "The 'New Breed' in American Churches," *Daedalus,* vol. 96, no. 1 (Winter 1967), p. 141.

12. J. Milton Yinger, "The Function and Control of Power in the Church in Relation to the Question of Unity and Disunity," *Institutionalism,* Division of Studies Bulletin, vol. 6, no. 1, World Council of Churches.

13. Mill, *Representative Government,* pp. 134-135.

14. Ibid., p. 136.

15. Erik H. Erikson, ed., *The Challenge of Youth* (Garden City, N.Y.: Doubleday & Company, Anchor Books, 1965), p. 83.

16. Yves M.-J. Congar, *Lay People in the Church* (New York: Newman Press, 1964; originally published London, 1957), p. 253.

17. Walter Bagehot, *The English Constitution* (Garden City, N.Y.: Doubleday & Company, Dolphin Books, originally published 1872), pp. 231-232.

18. Ibid., p. 232.

19. Mill, *Representative Government,* p. 124.

20. Ibid., pp. 124-125.